MISSION
NOT ACCOMPLISHED
How George Bush Lost
the War on Terrorism

William W. Turner

MISSION NOT ACCOMPLISHED
How George Bush Lost the War on Terrorism

William T. Turner
6/10/04

PENMARIN BOOKS
Roseville, California

Editorial Offices:	*Sales and Customer Service Offices:*
Penmarin Books	Midpoint Trade Books
1044 Magnolia Way	27 W. 20th Street, Suite 1102
Roseville, CA 95661	New York, NY 10011
	(212) 727-0190

Cover photos: Twin towers—Reuters/Steven James Silva; Bush—Reuters/ Jason Reed

Penmarin Books are available at special discounts for bulk purchases for premiums, sales promotions, or education. For details contact the Publisher or go to www.penmarin.com. On your letterhead, include information concerning the intended use of the books and how many you wish to purchase.

Visit our Website at **www.penmarin.com** for more information about this and other exciting titles, such as William Turner's memoirs, *Rearview Mirror: Looking Back at the FBI, the CIA and Other Tails.*

Printed in the United States of America
1 2 3 4 5 6 7 8 9 10   08 07 06 05 04

ISBN 1-883955-34-3

Library of Congress Control Number: 2004104443

Contents

CONTENTS

It's called Bannergate.

—CNBC anchor Brian Williams, November 3, 2003

Preface

The trophy hunt for Saddam Hussein ended abruptly in December 2003 when he was run to ground—literally—after eight months on the run following the fall of Baghdad. President George W. Bush hailed the capture as "Good riddance. The world is better off." As far as the war on terrorism was concerned, however, it was a non-event. Following the 9/11 attacks, the American people had commissioned the president to seek out Osama bin Laden, the evil genius behind the attacks, and destroy his al-Qaida terrorist network, and now, more than two years later, he was still at large, al-Qaida intact. The troops who found Saddam hiding in a hole reported he was not in possession of communications gear or any other paraphernalia that would suggest he had directed the cruel insurgency that would go on, exacting a tremendous toll in blood and money.

But it is Saddam, who had nothing to do with 9/11, who is in the dock being prosecuted. The trial undoubtedly will feature evidence of his genocidal crimes against the Kurds in northeastern Iraq after they aided Iran in the eight-year war of the 1980s, one in which the Reagan-Bush administration supplied weapons to Saddam (Donald Rumsfeld was dispatched to Baghdad to assure Saddam that his possession of chemical weapons would not affect his relations with the United States). And Saddam's mass crimes against the Shi'ite Muslims in the Basra area, who were encouraged to revolt after the

First Gulf War by the first President Bush, who abandoned them when they did. Not on the docket will be the 9/11 attacks. Although the Bush administration originally created the impression that Saddam was a co-perpetrator with bin Laden in the attacks—an indelible impression in the minds of many Americans—the links proved gossamer. Even Deputy Defense Secretary Paul Wolfowitz, one of the chief architects of the invasion of Iraq, came to admit on Laura Ingraham's conservative radio talk show that there was no convincing evidence to tie in Saddam with 9/11. The Iraqi dictator may have terrorized his own people, but he didn't export terrorism.

Missing from the dock was Osama bin Laden, who had pulled off by far the boldest and most catastrophic act of terrorism ever. Even the belated capture of bin Laden and his high command will not stop al-Qaida, which used the interregnum of the Iraq invasion to regroup and retrench as well as bond with independent terrorist units around the globe. Under pressure from the dominant neo-con caucus in his administration, most prominently Vice President Richard Cheney and Wolfowitz, to use the war on terrorism as an opportunity to topple Saddam, a goal they had sighted in on as long ago as 1998, Bush declared bin Laden "not important" and pulled out the paramilitary and intelligence assets, including spy satellites, from Afghanistan for the campaign against Iraq. As CIA Director George Tenet conceded in the wake of the worldwide rash of deadly bombings following the "regime change" in Baghdad, al-Qaida was back—with a vengeance.

The capture of Saddam Hussein was such a huge news story that it blotted out a budding Bush administration scandal. The president had no sooner consoled the families of the American war dead, declaring that they had died in a "noble and just cause," than in-your-face war profiteering by the Halliburton Company burst onto the scene. A giant oil services firm based in Houston, its chief executive officer had been Dick Cheney, who continued to receive millions of dollars in deferred compensation after he left to assume the vice presidency of the United States. So there was no mystery behind why the Pentagon, as the occupation began, had awarded Halliburton a no-bid, open-ended contract to rebuild Iraq's oil infrastructure that was estimated to have a potential price tag of $15.6 billion. All was going well with the deal by the time of Bush's abbreviated Thanksgiving junket to the Baghdad airport for a photo op with the troops while holding a plastic turkey provided by Kellogg Brown & Root (KBR), a wholly owned Halliburton subsidiary with a contract to feed the occupying army throughout Iraq. But *New York Times* reporter Douglas Jehl laid hands on Pentagon internal documents that showed that Halliburton's sweetheart deal had turned into a greedy gouging. In a front-page story December 12, 2003, Jehl reported that KBR overcharged the government by as much as $61 million for gasoline delivered from Kuwait at $2.63 a gallon, which was more than twice the going rate. At the same time, KBR was charging $28 per day per soldier for food that the troops complained was lousy, sometimes rotting, and often made them sick.

U.S. Representative Henry Waxman, a severe critic of the no-bid Halliburton contract, said that Jehl's article "confirmed what we've been knowing for months. Halliburton has been gouging taxpayers, and the White House has been letting them get away with it." In a move to isolate himself from the rip-off, Bush played the role of honest broker, saying that if the overcharges were confirmed, he would expect Halliburton to refund the $61 million. Then, with the apprehension of Saddam Hussein, the fog of war enshrouded the controversy. Halliburton never repaid the money, but simply bowed out of the oil delivery contract. "The task of transporting fuel into

Iraq was always understood by KBR to be temporary," a company spokesperson alibied. Nothing was said about the lousy food at an exorbitant $28 per day per soldier.

Nor did George H. W. Bush, the president's father, go unrewarded by the war. His vehicle to additional riches was the Carlyle Group, a private investment banking entity of which he holds the title Senior Advisor. As Oliver Burkeman and Julian Borger told it in *The Guardian* of London on October 31, 2001:

> [As] the Carlyle investors watched the World Trade Towers go down, the group's prospects went up. In running what its own marketing literature spookily calls "a vast, interlocking, global network of businesses and investment professionals" that operates within the so-called iron triangle of industry, government, and the military, the Carlyle Group leaves itself open to any number of conflicts of interest and stunning ironies. For example, it is hard to ignore the fact that Osama bin Laden's family members, who renounced their son ten years ago, stood to gain financially from the war being waged against him until late October, when public criticism of the relationship forced them to liquidate their holdings in the firm. Or consider that U.S. president George W. Bush is in a position to make budgetary decisions that could pad his father's bank account. But for the Carlyle Group, walking that narrow line is the art of doing business at the murky intersection of Washington politics, national security and private capital; mastering it has enabled the group to amass $12 billion in funds under management.

The Carlyle Group is heavily invested in major U.S. defense firms that manufacture tanks, airplanes and weapons systems, making it part of the military-industrial complex. Its leadership is wired to the federal government. The chairman and chief executive officer is Frank Carlucci, a secretary of defense and deputy director of the CIA under Reagan/Bush, and the senior counselor is James Baker III, secretary of state under the senior Bush. It was Baker, who now heads a Republican-connected Houston law firm, that led the Bush team which contested and won the Florida vote in the 2000 election. In December 2003 President Bush dispatched him on a mission to restructure postwar Iraq's foreign debt by persuading the owed countries to forgive all or part of the debt. Baker met with limited success, mainly because Bush, in an act of spite, had just barred France, Germany, Russia, China and Canada from new Iraqi contracts because they had opposed an invasion without U.N. authorization. But Baker's most cynical assignment is defending the Saudi Arabian monarchy, the Royal House of Saud, as well as the bin Laden family in an epic lawsuit brought by 9/11 victims' families that charges they funneled money to al-Qaida. The Saudi royal family and the bin Ladens were heavy-hitter investors in the Carlyle Group, having been recruited by George Bush the elder.

"How will President George W. Bush personally make millions (if not billions) from the War on Terror and Iraq?" Burkeman and Borger posed in their *Guardian* piece. "The old fashioned way. He'll inherit it."

George W. Bush cronies are also being cut in on the spoils of war in the here and now. No, not Kenneth Lay, who had become so close a buddy that Bush called him Kenny Boy; Lay's Enron Corporation had collapsed in scandal and he was a political pariah. In May 2003, as the invasion of Iraq ended and the occupation began, a new company, New Bridge Strategies, sprang into being in Washington. At its head was Joe Allbaugh, who had recently quit as the Bush-appointed director of the Federal Emergency Management Agency (FEMA), which was merged into the Department of Homeland Security. On the firm's Web site, Allbaugh is touted as "chief of staff to then-Gov. Bush of Texas and national campaign manager for the Bush-Cheney 2000 presidential campaign." Other New

Bridge officers numbered Edward Rogers Jr. and Lanny Griffith, lobbyists who were on the staff of the first President Bush and can still pick up the phone and call the White House. The Web site boasts: "The opportunities evolving in Iraq today are of such an unprecedented nature and scope that no other existing firm has the necessary skills and experience to be effective both in Washington, D.C., and on the ground in Iraq." Decoded, the pitch says we can exploit our singular Bush administration contacts to get you contracts paid for with taxpayers' money.

In his farewell address to the nation on January 17, 1961, ending eight years as president, General Dwight D. Eisenhower, the World War II hero and Republican icon, sounded a tocsin against the danger posed by an overly powerful military-industrial complex. "In the councils of government, we must guard against the acquisition of unwarranted influence, whether sought or unsought, by the military-industrial complex," he said. "The potential rise of misplaced power exists and will persist. We must never let the weight of this combination endanger our liberties or democratic processes. We should take nothing for granted. Only an alert and knowledgeable citizenry can compel the proper meshing of the huge industrial and military machinery of defense with our peaceful methods and goals, so that security and liberty can prosper together."

The wannabe warrior now in the White House—he never served in the armed forces of the United States—has caused General Eisenhower's worst fears to be realized. Bush converted the 9/11 attacks, which merited an intelligence campaign response against al-Qaida, into a shooting war with Iraq. He cracked down on our liberties, using dragnet tactics. He signaled a warcentric foreign policy with his "axis of evil" hype. He plunged the country into runaway debt by showering the Pentagon with billions of extra dollars and unprecedented authority, enabling its war contractors to reap enormous profits. Even the CIA, which is responsible for rooting out al-Qaida abroad, is now subordinate to the Pentagon. Bush has acquired a vested interest in war. It renders him, he thinks, irreplaceable as commander in chief.

In truth, he is eminently replaceable. Insinuations to the contrary, Saddam Hussein never was a threat to the American homeland, nor did he possess weapons of mass destruction as advertised. The war against him had nothing to do with national defense—it had to do with oil and the neocons' vision of American hegemony in commercially strategic corners of the earth. Osama bin Laden and his al-Qaida were—and remain—the American nightmare. Bush committed a monumental strategic blunder when he dubbed bin Laden "not important," sidetracked the war on terrorism, and marched on Baghdad. Al-Qaida emerged from the respite stronger and more motivated than ever, and augurs to be with us even after bin Laden is gone. This was illustrated over the 2003 Christmas holidays when a spike in "chatter" attributed to al-Qaida units led to cancellations of flights on both sides of the Atlantic and the interrogations of hundreds of passengers. Whether there was an actual plot in the works or it was part of al-Qaida's war of nerves designed to spread fear and inflict economic damage, the psychological impact was immense. The message was: Al-Qaida is back.

Early in 2004, Bush launched an election year "spring offensive" in Afghanistan to kill or capture bin Laden, but by that time bin Laden also was no more than a trophy. He was holed up in an emeritus status, communicating only by courier, and leaving the operations of a resurgent al-Qaida to new blood. The war on al-Qaida and its allies cannot be won with tanks, bombers, Humvees and flotillas. The network transcends borders, encircling the globe, and is sub rosa. The war on terrorism must necessarily be a silent war, fought by counterintelligence professionals. It is a battle of wits, a sophisticated exercise aimed at ferreting out and neutralizing "sleeper cells," the operational arms of al-Qaida, wherever they may be. It requires dogged imagination, creativity and inventiveness— exactly the opposite of the regimented military mind. In this occult demimonde, there are no bands playing "Hail to the Chief," no photo ops with aircraft carriers and dummy Thanksgiving turkeys.

When George W. Bush lost sight of the mission, America and the world became infinitely more dangerous places.

William W. Turner
San Rafael, California
April 2004

About the Author

William Turner was a special agent with the FBI from 1951 to 1961, during which time he served as a counterintelligence specialist against the Soviet KGB and GRU. He later became a National Wiretap Commission investigator in 1975. Turner is a life member of Veterans of Foreign Wars.

When he left the Bureau in 1961, he turned to investigative journalism. His work has appeared in *The Nation, Playboy, New West, The Progressive, Penthouse* and *Scanlon's Monthly,* among other publications, and he was a senior editor of *Ramparts* magazine. His many books include *Hoover's FBI; The Police Establishment; The 10-Second Jailbreak* (with Warren Hinckle and Eliot Asinof); *The Assassination of Robert Kennedy* (with Jonn Christian); *Deadly Secrets: The CIA-Mafia War Against Castro and the Assassination of JFK* (with Warren Hinckle); and *Rearview Mirror: Looking Back at the FBI, the CIA and Other Tails.* A number of them have been published in Spanish, Russian, French, Japanese, Polish and United Kingdom editions.

Considered a top expert on the FBI, the CIA, assassinations and the paramilitary right, Turner has appeared on many TV shows and lectured widely on these subjects. After the September 11 attacks, he consulted as a counterintelligence analyst for CNN and CNN International.

INTRODUCTION

On May Day 2003 a peacock-proud President George W. Bush, garbed in a flight suit, stood on the deck of the aircraft carrier *Abraham Lincoln* and pronounced major combat in the invasion of Iraq at an end. Behind him, strung from the bridge of the huge vessel, was a banner reading: MISSION ACCOMPLISHED. Bush had sold the invasion as an integral part of his war on terrorism.

Six months later, in October, Secretary of Defense Donald Rumsfeld drafted an internal memorandum stating that more than two years after the attacks of September 11, 2001, it remained unclear whether the United States was winning the war on terrorism or if the ranks of Islamic militants were swelling faster than the U.S. government could stop them. "Today, we lack metrics to know whether we are winning or losing the war on terror," the memo, reported by *USA Today*, said. "Is our current situation such that the harder we work, the behinder we get?"

The memo was what had become known in the Pentagon as a Rumsfeld "snowflake," posing questions to prompt soul-searching by his subordinates. He concluded that there had been "mixed results" in the battle against the al-Qaida network responsible for the 9/11 attacks, and that the military operations in Afghanistan—where a punitive expedition had been mounted against the Taliban regime, which had harbored al-Qaida's supreme commander, Osama bin Laden—and Iraq will be a "long, hard slog." Although Rumsfeld wrote that despite the considerable pressure that had been put on al-Qaida a "great many remain at large," and that "reasonable progress" had been made in tracking down leaders of the ousted Iraqi government—remember the deck of playing cards?—"somewhat slower" strides had been made in running to ground the Taliban hierarchy (in fact, a guerrilla war in Afghanistan had recently flared).

Left unsaid by Rumsfeld was the embarrassing fact that at the time Osama bin Laden as well as the Iraqi despot, Saddam Hussein, had not been killed or captured, as Bush had vowed.

It was a telling memorandum for the usually cocksure Rumsfeld to author. The desperation he felt to find a solution was indicated by his musing that "it is not possible to change (the Defense Department) fast enough to successfully fight the war on terror; an alternative might be to try to fashion a new institution, either within (the Pentagon) or elsewhere—one that seamlessly focuses the capabilities of several departments and agencies on this key problem."

What Rumsfeld didn't comprehend was that the solution lay not in his venue, military force, but in counterintelligence effectiveness. Al-Qaida and its affiliates around the globe are not nation-states with defined borders and military establishments. They are integrated underground networks transcending national frontiers, every bit as crafty as the Viet Cong guerrillas during the Vietnam War. They strike at a time and place of their choosing, maintaining the initiative. Generals, bombers and tanks are of no use against them. Instead of conventional military operations, the terrorists wage a silent war—punctuated by their weapon of choice, the high-explosive bomb (the hijacked 9/11 airliners were turned into flying bombs). David Benjamin, a terrorism official on the National Security Council during the Clinton administration and currently a senior fellow at the Center for Strategic and International Studies, made the point: "We have an Iraq policy but not a radical Islam policy. Iraq was not a terrorism problem before we invaded." The invasion, which was a part of the war on terrorism only in the minds of Bush and Rumsfeld, left a destabilized Iraq that Bush called a "magnet for terrorists." Chaos reigned. The tempo of bombings rivaled that of Rumsfeld's "Shock and Awe" campaign. Al-Qaida emerged from the conflict stronger than ever, taking advantage of Bush's preoccupation with Iraq to regroup and expand. In what will be recorded as one of history's most egregious blunders, Bush pronounced bin Laden "not important" as he turned his sights onto Saddam Hussein. Egyptian President Hosni Mubarak had warned Bush that a preemptive strike against Iraq would create millions of new Muslim radicals in the region, a hundred new bin Ladens. It had come to pass.

On the morning of the 9/11 attacks I arrived at the San Francisco airport destined for France only to find all air traffic stopped indefinitely. No sooner had I arrived back home than the phone rang. Radio station WECH in Michigan was on the line. Several months earlier I had been on the air with host John St. Augustine discussing intelligence matters, in particular the FBI's National Security Division, which was responsible for counterintelligence and counterterrorism, largely identical techniques. As an FBI agent in the early 1960s, I had been a counterintelligence specialist against the Soviet KGB and GRU (Red Army Intelligence), and had tracked the progress, or lack of it, of the U.S. intelligence agencies ever since. On the WECH program, I had pointed out that under Director J. Edgar Hoover the G-men earned their reputation going after such Public Enemies as George "Machine Gun" Kelly and John Dillinger. But counterintelligence was the polar opposite of the fast-paced, adrenaline-inducing criminal arena where headlines were the norm and prosecution the goal. It is a nuanced, dreary needle-in-a-haystack process that might drag on for years and at that not eventuate in a prosecution. Many agents shun it as too complex and intellectual with no instant rewards. Yet the FBI remained geared toward criminal work, with counterintelligence playing second fiddle. The recent Wen Ho Lee espionage case in Santa Fe and the Robert Hanssen case in Washington—for years he had been a Russian mole inside the FBI's most sensitive operations—evidenced how dysfunctional the National Security Division was. A whole new era, the same old FBI. In an appearance on C-SPAN2 Book TV program two months before 9/11, I spelled out the Bureau's irreversible shortcomings in the counterintelligence field, and exhorted, "It's up to Congress to form a commission to start over with the FBI."

So when WECH called that tragic morning, I was appalled not that the attacks had taken place on American soil—there had been a truck bombing of the World Trade Center in 1993 that claimed six lives—but at their brazenness and scale. Four civilian jetliners hijacked in flight. Two were flown into the World Trade Center's twin towers, one was slammed into the Pentagon, and the fourth, with the White House or CIA headquarters as the probable target, plunged into a Pennsylvania field after passengers struggled to wrest control. The death toll, I knew, must be horrific. It was a prima facie case of a massive intelligence agency failure, since a plan that intricate perforce took years to organize.

4

The question that St. Augustine of WECH posed was: What do you think of President Bush's capability to handle a crisis of this magnitude? I knew a little about Bush's career path, and it wasn't reassuring. He had begun a business career in Texas with his own small oil company, Arbusto Energy (*arbusto* means "shrub" in Spanish), with the aid of a $50,000 investment from family friend James Bath. It is highly ironical that Bath was the sole U.S. representative for Salem bin Laden, a wealthy Saudi Arabian businessman and brother of Osama bin Laden, and there were indications, now denied by Bush, that bin Laden money wound up in the Arbusto bank account. When tough times in the oil patch had Arbusto teetering, he merged with Spectrum 7, another marginal firm. He guided Spectrum 7 to the brink of bankruptcy, only to be rescued, in what would become a pattern, by Friends of Poppy, as his father was known to intimates. Harken Oil & Gas bought out Spectrum 7 in 1986, giving Bush cash, stock and an executive position. In 1990, acting on inside information, he sold his Harken stock just before the firm announced financial bad news and the stock price cratered. His insider trading and failure to report the sale triggered an SEC probe, but his father was president at the time and the SEC closed the case with an ambiguous statement that it didn't intend to prosecute. In a move arranged by another FOP, Bush parlayed his profits from the Harken sale into an equity in the Texas Rangers baseball franchise. But on the field the team continued its losing ways, prompting Bush to remark that the dumbest move he made was trading Sammy Sosa to Chicago. Nevertheless, he walked away with a sizable profit when he sold his interest.

Bush's political career is also checkered. His first run, for U.S. Congress in 1978, was stage-managed by Karl Rove, the crafty, ruthless operator who had handled Poppy from the beginning. Although he lost that election, Bush went on to win two terms as governor of Texas by trading on his family name with FOP money. His six years in the state capital—he seldom ventured to Dallas, Houston and other sizable cities because his handlers knew he couldn't think on his feet and feared to let him loose unscripted—were unremarkable. He was not known as a workhorse, spending much time jogging on paths near the capitol building, but the fact that the power in Texas is vested in the state legislature, not the governorship, may account for his abundance of free time. Nevertheless, he claimed credit for advancing education in Texas, overlooking the fact that the Houston school system became a shambles under his tenure. In running for the Republican nomination for president in Campaign 2000, Bush became the complete political animal when, after being trounced by Senator John McCain in the New Hampshire primary, he used Bob Jones University as a bully pulpit to shamelessly attack McCain in the succeeding South Carolina primary. Since the institution is famously prejudicial to blacks, Jews and Catholics—Bob Jones once called the Catholic Church "that harlot church"—Bush obviously intended to appeal to the state's bigot bloc of voters (I admit that as a Catholic I resented the ploy).

What I found disturbing about Bush, insofar as his ability to cope with complex problems such as the ramifications of 9/11, was the shallowness of his life experience, which is to say oilcentric. Until he became president, he had never had the broadening experience of traveling overseas except for a family vacation in China in 1975. He saw things in black and white, not being sophisticated enough to perceive the shades in between, and, he told journalist Bob Woodward, made decisions based on "gut instinct." His borderline xenophobia was on display less than three months after his inauguration when an American spy plane patrolling the Chinese coast collided

6

with a People's Republic fighter jet and crash-landed on Hainan Island. Waving a fist at China, Bush unconditionally demanded the immediate return of the plane and its crew. Chinese President Jiang Zemin must have looked on bemusedly at Bush's histrionics. The release of captured spies is something that is negotiated—after experts have had a chance to examine the sensitive electronics on board.

Although Clinton's National Security Advisor Sandy Berger had handed over the dossier on Osama bin Laden to Bush's NSA, Condoleezza Rice, the new administration did not appear to put terrorism on the front burner. Rice, an academic who had composed papers on the evils of the Soviet system for a conservative think tank, was unschooled on the subject and was in fact busy crafting a new isolationist, unilateral foreign policy based on America's status as the lone remaining superpower. Attorney General John Ashcroft concentrated on crimes such as child pornography that offended his sense of religiosity. Bush's appointee for the vacant job of FBI director was ex-U.S. Attorney Robert Mueller, who for twenty-one years had prosecuted ordinary crimes with no experience in intelligence matters. Meanwhile John O'Neill, the blustery FBI agent in command of the National Security Division in New York who had led the investigation of the bombing of the USS *Cole* in Yemeni waters, was giving speeches warning that al-Qaida would soon be dropping a big one on the American homeland. Bush had available a 1999 report prepared for the National Intelligence Council asserting that "Suicide bombers belonging to al-Qaida's Martyrdom Battalion could crash-land an aircraft packed with explosives into the Pentagon, the headquarters of the Central Intelligence Agency, or the White House." On August 6, 2001, with 9/11 a month off, Bush received a CIA briefing delivered by Condoleezza Rice at his Crawford, Texas, ranch, where he was vacationing, that an al-Qaida plot was pending to commandeer airliners, envisioning suicide crashes. When *CBS News* broke the story of the Crawford briefing after 9/11, Bush alibied that he could not "envision" al-Qaida cadres hijacking civilian airliners and flying them into strategic buildings. Even after the National Security Agency, on the eve of 9/11, picked up a spike in al-Qaida electronic traffic with a message suggesting that something big was coming down the next day, no order went out to the Federal Aviation Administration to tighten security checks on passengers.

So Bush knew that al-Qaida had the method and means—and was just waiting for the opportunity. He failed to recognize the neon signs. He had flunked his terrorism test.

It was with this in mind that I answered John St. Augustine on WECH, when he asked what I thought of Bush's capability to handle the 9/11 crisis, "Well, he's incompetent, but Americans will rally around him because he's president just like they rallied around his father in Gulf War I." I indicated that Bush was the wrong president at the wrong time. But all of that was lost in the torrent of patriotic fervor that engulfed the nation in the aftermath, a climate that equated criticism of the president with treason. Bush spokesman Ari Fleischer intimidated the media by saying, "Watch what you write." The shibboleth out of the White House was biblical: He who is not with me is against me. A dark shadow of silence moved across the land, as Bush assumed the role of commander in chief, swaggering as if his face would one day be carved into Mount Rushmore. Right-wing media bobbleheads monopolized the airwaves, savagely attacking the few who had the gumption to criticize the president. But that was then, and this is now. Bush has fouled up so royally that freedom of the press has been restored.

The theme of this book is that Bush is a loose cannon who lost the war on terrorism he was finally tasked with waging by the events of 9/11. He began losing it the day after when he secretly instructed, at the request of the Saudi Arabian government, the FBI to chaperone members of the royal family and Osama bin Laden's relatives onto evacuation planes when all flights had been ordered grounded. His special treatment—he and his father had long-standing financial ties to the Saudis—aborted questioning that might have led to the discovery of al-Qaida's money conduits. Within days, he was stampeding a supine Congress to rush through a loosely written USA Patriot Act, the greatest threat to civil liberties in the republic since the Justice Department's notorious Red Raids of 1919–1920 following a wave of bombings gratuitously attributed to anarchists. Under pressure to do something positive, Bush pilfered from Senator Joseph Lieberman the idea of consolidating many units of government tangentially concerned with preventing terrorist acts such as the Coast Guard and Immigration & Naturalization Service into a cabinet-level superbureaucracy; he called it the Department of Homeland Defense and named a politician to head it. It was nothing more than a feel-good move, since the smuggling of contraband and people remains impossible to prevent, as witness the narcotics trafficking quandary. The real homeland defense lies in the ability of the FBI and CIA to ferret out terrorist cells and neutralize them before they can strike. Although both failed miserably to avert the 9/11 attacks, Bush has neglected to revamp them, leaving the homeland vulnerable to another Big One.

The Iraq diversion from the war on terrorism after the Taliban turkey shoot gave the terrorist groupings, with the pressure off, a window of opportunity to regroup. Toppling the Baghdad regime had long been a goal of the neocons now positioned in the Bush administration, notably Paul Wolfowitz and Richard Perle, as part of their ambitious Project for a New American Century to gain hegemony in strategic regions of the globe. As Seymour M. Hersh put it in *The New Yorker* for October 27, 2003: "By early March, 2002, a former White House official told me, it was understood by many in the White House that the President had decided, in his own mind, to go to war. The undeclared decision had a devastating impact on the continuing struggle against terrorism. The Bush administration took many intelligence operations that had been aimed at Al Queda and other terrorist groups around the world and redirected them to the Persian Gulf. Linguists and special operatives were abruptly reassigned, and several ongoing antiterrorism intelligence programs were curtailed."

Al-Qaida and its affiliates emerged from the Iraq hiatus resurgent, carrying out a wave of bombings around the world. Bush, who had a beatific vision of his advancing legions being greeted with tossed flowers by the population, could only watch in disbelief when, in October 2003, the toll of GIs killed since his May Day victory speech climbed over the two hundred mark. There was widespread looting and disorder, and resistance at home to the $87 billion price tag he put on rebuilding the destruction he had wrought. He had to go cup in hand for contributions from nations he had insulted only months earlier when they opposed his plans for a preemptive strike. Worse still, his policies had precipitated a drop in the opinion polls, which didn't augur well for Campaign 2004.

In a Rose Garden news conference, the president put the best possible face on the mess he had created. While Iraq was still a dangerous place and it would take patience to stabilize it, he said, "the world is more peaceful and more free under my leadership." And that, he announced, would be a cornerstone of his reelection campaign.

Braced by a reporter about the MISSION ACCOMPLISHED banner displayed on the *Abraham Lincoln* on May Day, Bush bristled, saying that the banner was placed there by the carrier's crew members, not White House staff. As the conference ended, a White House spokeswoman emerged to issue a correction. The crew had asked the White House to have the banner made, which it had a vendor do, and the crew put it up.

Senator Joe Lieberman had the last mocking word on that one. The president's assertion, he said, was "another banner day in George Bush's quest to bring honor and integrity to the White House. If he wanted to prove he has trouble leveling with the American people, mission accomplished."

1

MISSION NOT ACCOMPLISHED

Decked out in a flight suit, his hair mussed by the wind, George W. Bush stood ramrod proud on the deck of the aircraft carrier *Abraham Lincoln* off San Diego on May 1, 2003. Behind him was a large banner proclaiming: MISSION ACCOMPLISHED. The commander in chief was there, he said, to announce that major combat in the war against Iraq was over. Standing deferentially to his side was his national security advisor, Condoleezza Rice, costumed in a flight suit, earmuffs and goggles, looking every bit as ludicrous as Michael Dukakis with his helmeted head sticking out of a tank turret during his failed 1988 bid for the presidency against the elder George Bush.

It was all Kodak perfect. The *Abraham Lincoln* had been swung around so that only the vast expanse of sea, not the San Diego skyline, would be the backdrop. Hundreds of sailors were mustered on deck like props in a Cecil B. DeMille film epic. Bush had been flown to the carrier in a Viking jet, which made a dramatic tailhook landing. Asked beforehand why the president wasn't simply helicoptered out, White House spokesman Ari Fleischer at first explained that helicopters didn't have the range to reach the carrier. When that proved untrue, he switched to a story that Bush wanted to experience the rush of flying, and might even take the controls himself part of the way.

For Bush, a glutton for photo ops, this was the mother of them all, a theatrical tour de force that would establish him as the nation's Top Gun, providing a canister of film clips that could be used during Campaign 2004 to trump such troubling issues as the state of the economy. But no sooner had he returned to shore in a suit and tie than the wretched excess began to backfire. Angry, sarcastic letters to the editors of newspapers across the country accused Bush of shameless grandstanding, of pulling off a not-so-cheap publicity stunt, of strutting like a military martinet, of jingoism in the extreme. And a dirty little secret from his past, one that his handlers had persuaded Al Gore not to exploit during Campaign 2000, was dredged up: The president was a Vietnam War draft dodger, a "chicken hawk" who was all for the conflict but ducked fighting it. In 1968, as American troops were dying at the rate of some 350 a week, his student deferment was about to expire. So, in a less than patriotic moment, he walked into the Houston office of the Texas Air National Guard, which at the time was guaranteed not to deploy beyond the state's borders, to sign up. Although no slots were open, young Bush was accepted. It was, as General Colin Powell put it in his memoirs, a case of "a son of the privileged" — his father was then a U.S. congressman — finagling shelter from the draft. Worse still, he was AWOL a good part of the time. Eric Zorn of the *Chicago Tribune* vented in his column that in May 1972 Bush "sought a transfer from Houston, where he flew F-102s on weekends, to a unit in Montgomery, Ala. There he worked on the U.S. Senate campaign of his father's friend, and, records indicate, blew off his military obligations. Bush failed to take his annual flight physical in 1972 so Guard officials grounded him, the story went. He never flew again and received an early discharge to go to graduate school. His final officer-efficiency report from May 1973 noted only that supervisors hadn't seen him or heard from him." The *New York Times*' Paul Krugman checked in that "Bush, who appears to have skipped a year of the National Guard service that kept him out of Vietnam, is now emphasizing his flying experience. There was a time when patriotic Americans from both parties would have denounced any president who tried to take political advantage of his role as commander in chief. But that, it seems, was another country."

It can be said that while Bush declared a military victory on May 1, 2003, that day also marked his losing of the war on terrorism. Only days after the 9/11 attacks, Bush locked onto Osama bin Laden and his terrorist network al-Qaida as the perpetrators. In his best cowboy style, the president vowed to "git" bin Laden and "bring him back dead or alive." U.S. intelligence agencies had fixed the location of bin Laden and his high command as in the Tora Bora mountain caves in eastern Afghanistan near the Pakistan frontier. The situation begged for a surgical strike by an elite commando group such as the Army's Delta Force to seal off and search the caves. But Bush dawdled, electing to first defeat the Taliban, an ultraorthodox ruling sect that had harbored bin Laden and his training camps. The Taliban armed forces were in fact a ragtag militia with black turbans. They were poorly armed with old rifles and, wags said, a lone hang glider as an air force. It was more a guerrilla band than fighting machine. Bush sent troops to overwhelm the Taliban, then had them wait while a warlord's Northern Alliance irregulars geared up to lead the advance. Once fighting started, it was over within short order, with Taliban remnants fleeing into the hills to form a resistance movement. It is a measure of how lopsided hostilities were that as many journalists were killed as troops. By the time British marines searched the Tora Bora caves in December, bin Laden and his retinue had vanished.

With no prize catch, Bush dismissed Osama bin Laden as "not important" and turned his sights onto Iraq with its visible villain, Saddam Hussein, defined borders, depleted army—and oil. He had been turned in that direction for reasons that had nothing to do with terrorism. In his State of the Union speech in January 2002, Bush with rhetorical flourish pointed his finger at an "axis of evil"— Iraq, Iran and North Korea—that actually had little to do with one another. It had long been a dream of a consortium of power-elite hard-liners to transform America's supremacy of culture, economy, technology and military might into a neo-Roman Empire pursuing a unilateral foreign policy under the mantra "peace through strength." The aim was to wrest control of strategic regions of the world through preemptive strikes if necessary. The charter architect of this doctrine was Richard Cheney, who in 1992, after serving as George H. W. Bush's secretary of defense, repaired to a hunting lodge near Greybull, Wyoming, and drafted the first blueprint. The doctrine matured during the Clinton years to the point where, in 1997, it was formalized into the Project for the New American Century (PNAC), a think tank subsidized by the defense industry, oil and gas behemoths, and conservative foundations. In addition to Cheney, PNAC's leadership hawks included now-Secretary of Defense Donald Rumsfeld, his deputy Paul Wolfowitz, and Richard Perle, a member of the Defense Policy Board, which is an advisory panel to the Pentagon composed of prominent national defense figures. In September 2000, the PNAC issued a comprehensive manifesto entitled "Rebuilding America's Defenses: Strategies, Forces and Resources for a New Century" that called for a quantum leap in military spending, the establishment of permanent military bases in the Middle East and Central Asia, regime change in nations that refused to comply, abrogation of pesky international treaties, hegemony over global energy sources, militarization of outer space, and the option to utilize nuclear weapons to realize American goals. It would be, as John Kennedy had warned, a Pax Americana thrust upon the world. The stick and the stick.

A regime change in Iraq, with its strategic location and black gold, was on the neoconservatives' calendar well before George Bush assumed the presidency in January 2001. The opportunity presented itself when the Afghan campaign ended. As revealed in the July 2003 *Vanity Fair* magazine, Paul Wolfowitz was instrumental in convincing Bush to target Iraq. According to a magazine source, Wolfowitz told the president: "Think about the fact that the second largest city in Iraq"—Basra—"is full of Shia who hate Saddam." Consider too, that Basra lies "within 60 kilometers of the Kuwaiti border and within 60 percent of Iraq's total oil production." For the petro-president, that argument stuck. (Ironically, when the war started, Basra held out to the end. The Shi'ite population remembered that after Gulf War I the senior Bush encouraged them to revolt, then stood idly by as Saddam slaughtered thousands.) To boot, Bush had long wanted personal revenge against Hussein for allegedly plotting to assassinate his father during an honorific visit to Kuwait after leaving the presidency.

Having made the decision to go to war for the oil, Bush struggled to find a casus belli he could sell to the American people. Interviewed by *Vanity Fair*, Wolfowitz admitted that from the outset, contrary to repeated claims by the White House, Iraq's supposed cache of WMD had never been the most compelling reason. "For bureau-cratic reasons we settled on one issue, weapons of mass destruc-tion," he said, "because it was the one reason everyone could agree on." This of course had nothing to do with the war on terrorism, since there was nothing credible to tie Hussein into the 9/11 attacks. Yet the White House repeated the charge so often that a majority of Americans was mesmerized into believing that Hussein as well as bin Laden was implicated. They only offered as "evidence" that a purported member of the network was treated at a Baghdad hospi-tal for a leg injury and that an al-Qaida contingent was based in north Iraq. Left unsaid was the fact that the area in question was an autonomous region under the control of the Kurds, who opposed the Baghdad regime. In what should have finished off the al-Qaida angle, the BBC in London, citing a British intelligence source, re-ported that several years earlier Osama bin Laden had approached Hussein about an alliance but was summarily rejected on grounds that culturally and politically they had nothing in common. But the putative al-Qaida link to 9/11 was floated when White House believability was sky high.

As Wolfowitz revealed, however, Bush and his brain trust settled on WMD as the main selling point to convince Americans that Hussein posed a clear and present danger to the nation. The hang-up was that there was no proof that Iraq, which had been contained for a decade by U.N. sanctions and scrutiny, currently possessed a WMD cache. Bush tried to hype it by contending that Iraq had developed a delivery system in the form of unmanned aerial ve-hicles (UAVs). "We are concerned that Iraq is exploring ways of using these UAVs for missions targeting the United States," he in-toned. It was pure bunkum. The UAVs had a range of three hun-dred miles, not sufficient to reach Tel Aviv much less Manhattan, and could not carry much of a payload. Nor did nations such as France and Germany, which were also threatened by al-Qaida and geographically more proximate to the Middle East, feel that Saddam was a menace.

At the instigation of the United States, Dr. Hans Blix, the Swedish chief U.N. weapons inspector, and his team began to scour Iraq for WMD. When they had come up empty after several weeks and Bush scoffed that they were the victims of a shell game, Saddam invited the CIA to come into the country and conduct its own search. Bush ignored the invitation, perhaps due to his lack of confidence in the Agency's ability—or willingness—to produce a plausible WMD scenario. The CIA was drawing a blank in coming up with anything of note through its own intelligence sources, and its professional analysts at the Langley, Virginia, headquarters were resisting turning creative (Christian Westermann, a State Department expert on chemical and biological weapons, would testify before Congress that he felt pressured to alter his reports to conform with the administration's line). The pressure was largely coming from Vice President Richard Cheney, the administration's point man on Iraq. According to the *Washington Post* on June 5, 2003, "Cheney and his most senior aide made multiple trips to the CIA over the past year to question analysts studying Iraq's weapons programs." Still drawing millions of dollars in deferred compensation from the Halliburton Company, a giant oil services firm, Cheney had a personal stake in overthrowing Hussein. The invasion of Iraq had hardly ended before Halliburton's Kellogg Brown & Root subsidiary was awarded a $7.5 billion no-bid contract to rebuild the infrastructure. It was reminiscent of a sweetheart deal President Lyndon B. Johnson handed Houston-based Brown & Root in 1964 when he escalated the Vietnam War. LBJ bamboozled Congress that the Tonkin Bay incident, in which North Vietnamese patrol craft supposedly opened fire on U.S. destroyers, was for real (it was later proved false). With war powers in hand, he gave George and Herman Brown, the owners of Brown & Root who were his seminal political sponsors, a huge no-bid contract to construct the sprawling Cam Ranh Bay base.

With the CIA reporting literal truth, the role of spinmeister was turned over to a small recondite Pentagon intelligence shop called the Office of Special Plans that had been set up by Paul Wolfowitz in the wake of the 9/11 attacks. According to Seymour M. Hersh in *The New Yorker* of May 12, 2003, the shop is run by a pair of long-time neocons, Douglas Feith and Abram Shulsky, who self-mockingly call themselves the Cabal. They usurped the Pentagon's established Defense Intelligence Agency. W. Patrick Lang, the former chief of Middle East intelligence at the DIA, told Hersh: "The Pentagon has banded together to dominate the government's foreign policy, and they've pulled it off. . . . The DIA has been intimidated and beaten to a pulp. And there's no guts at all in the CIA." The Office of Special Plans interviewed several Iraqi defectors, a breed notorious for saying what their handlers want them to say, and put the appropriate spin on the findings of the CIA, which was bumped from its traditional role as the White House's primary intelligence adviser. As a result, the Pentagon was calling the shots in American foreign policy. A playbook authored by the Office of Special Plans was given to Secretary of State Colin Powell by Dick Cheney to present before the General Assembly of the United Nations to justify the impending war. According to *U.S. News & World Report*, Powell was so incensed that the material was weak and insubstantial that he threw the pages in the air and yelled, "I'm not reading this bullshit!"

But the good general did read the bullbleep before the U.N. General Assembly. Eight days earlier, Bush in the course of his 2003 State of the Union address had uttered the infamous sixteen words, "The British government has learned that Saddam Hussein recently sought significant quantities of uranium from Africa." He elaborated that there was documentation that the small African nation of Niger had shipped 500 tons of "yellowcake" uranium oxide to Iraq, which, coupled with an intercepted shipment of aluminum rods supposedly for use in a nuclear weapons program, raised the chimera of an Iraqi nuclear weapons program. Afterward the International Atomic Energy Agency exposed the documents as crude cut-and-paste forgeries on the letterhead of a Niger official who left office in 1989, and the aluminum rods as unfit for nuclear use. An IAEA official told Seymour Hersh of *The New Yorker* that the documents "could be spotted [as fake] by someone using Google on the Internet."

After the war, Bush continued to insist that the Niger uranium story was true. His pretensions so frustrated a former ambassador to African countries named Joseph C. Wilson that he wrote an op-ed piece in the *New York Times* on July 5, 2003, spilling the beans. In February 2002, Wilson said, the CIA commissioned him to go to Africa to check out reports received by Cheney that Iraq was purchasing uranium from Niger. He came back to say that it was all nonsense. In his *Times* article, Wilson accused the administration of "misrepresenting the facts on an issue that was fundamental justification for going to war." Six days later, CIA Director George Tenet fell on his sword, issuing a statement that "the President had every reason to believe that the text presented to him was sound." Tenet claimed he had approved the Niger account, which was his mistake. After an interval sufficient to allow it to sink in to the public that the CIA was culpable, Bush uttered a Trumanesque "the buck stops here."

But that was not the end of it—there remained to chop off the head of the messenger. On July 14 conservative columnist Robert Novak, quoting an unnamed senior administration official, disclosed that Wilson's wife was a CIA undercover operative. The leak seemed aimed not only at payback but intimidating other potential whistle-blowers. But this time the administration, perhaps unwittingly, had gone over the top. In the 1970s, as the result of the assassination of the CIA station chief in Athens after his name had appeared in a leftist publication, Congress passed the Intelligence Identities Protection Act, which made it a felony to out a clandestine agent who had served overseas in the past five years. Wilson's wife, a striking blonde named Valerie Plame, fit that bill. Not only was her career in jeopardy, so was her life and the lives of the informants she had run in the Middle East.

The story caused a furor. Wilson himself suspected Karl Rove, the President's cutthroat political operative who jump-started the political careers of the Bushes père and fils. In 1992 Rove was fired from the Bush-Quayle campaign in Texas for leaking an internal shake-up to Novak. Others suggested Dick Cheney, who had started the Niger affair. One thing was certain: White House staffers don't wear Birkenstocks; they are a highly disciplined and secretive crew who wouldn't think of leaking on their own, so the inspiration and authorization had to come from the level of a Rove or Cheney. But we may never know. Bush rejected out of hand an independent special counsel to investigate, opting instead to put it in the hands of Attorney General John Ashcroft, whose appointment was recommended to Bush by Karl Rove. You can't ask a rabbit to deliver a carrot.

But the leakage inflicted the biggest damage of all on the intelligence war on terrorism. It compromised the CIA's ability to recruit and maintain agents on the ground overseas because their security cannot be guaranteed.

In his delivery before the U.N. General Assembly, Colin Powell omitted the Niger allegation his boss had made little more than a week before. Instead he brandished a test tube containing a white powder he identified as anthrax, which causes an infectious disease in humans usually from contact with animal hair, hides or waste. He intimated that anthrax was in Iraq's bioweapons inventory, but didn't explain whether Hussein possessed the intricate knowledge to weaponize it. Powell's intended tour de force, however, was a set of photo blowups, taken by a spy satellite, showing two open truck trailers with some Rube Goldberg plumbing that had been identified by a human intelligence source, presumably a defector, as mobile bioweapons labs. Saddam was playing a shell game with the trailers, Powell charged, moving them from site to site to fool the U.N. inspectors. Later, when the U.S. invasion force moved close to Baghdad, the trailers were discovered. They had no sterilization component, a requisite for biological manufacture, and testing found no trace of anthrax, sarin or any other toxin. A London news source disclosed that the trailers were used to generate hydrogen for spotter balloons that were part of a British artillery system sold to Iraq years ago. This was subsequently confirmed by the Pentagon's Defense Intelligence Agency.

The United Nations found Powell's smoke-and-mirrors skit unconvincing, and pitched for more time to allow weapons inspectors to finish their task. After all, in 1995 a defector, General Hussein Kamel, told Rolf Ekeus, executive chairman of the U.N. inspection teams who had been instrumental in imposing sanctions on Iraq,

"All weapons, biological, chemical, missile, nuclear, were destroyed."
(Kamel, Saddam's son-in-law, was lured back to Baghdad, then summarily executed.) But Bush pronounced himself "impatient," while
Donald Rumsfeld sneered at France and Germany, which led the
call for more time, as "old Europe." In fact, major players like Russia and China wanted to allow the inspectors to finish their job, as
did neighbors Canada and Mexico. These countries weren't against
the use of force as such, and if WMD were found, stood ready to
agree to a regime change. But the White House neocons, committed to their expansionist agenda, couldn't take the risk that the inspectors would come up dry. The countdown began as Bush
dismissed the United Nations as irrelevant and proclaimed that the
war would be waged by a "coalition of the willing"—for all practical purposes the United States and Britain. Huge antiwar demonstrations erupted all over the globe, including Britain, where there
was a reservoir of resentment over George Bush leading Prime Minister Tony Blair by the nose into an unnecessary war. The list of the
leaders who counseled against it was long and prestigious, ranging
from the elder Bush's national security advisor Brent Scowcroft and
General Wesley Clark, chief of the action against Serbia, to Nelson
Mandela and Pope John Paul II, who deemed it "unjust."

The most prescient advice came from the president of Egypt,
Hosni Mubarak, who knew the Arab mind. An invasion of Iraq,
Mubarak warned, would create millions of new Islamic radicals, a
hundred new bin Ladens.

On March 17, 2003, Bush enhanced his stature as a fabulist when
he claimed that intelligence reports left no doubt Iraq possessed
WMD. After a slight delay caused by Turkey's refusal to accept a $3
billion bribe to allow American troops to jump off from its soil, the
"Shock and Awe" bombing began. The war on the ground proved

to be no more than a series of skirmishes lasting three weeks. No Iraqi fighters took to the skies, no elite Republican Guard divisions blocked the road to Baghdad. The Iraqi forces melted into the cities, doffed their uniforms, and became guerrilla fighters. Saddam had harbored no illusions that his conventional forces could defeat the overwhelming American power.

From his prewar rhetoric about liberating the Iraqi people and bringing them democracy, it seems clear that Bush believed that his troops would be greeted with open arms by the locals. He badly miscalculated. The sullen majority didn't want foreign invaders installing an Enron-style democracy in their ancient land of Mesopotamia. For centuries they had resisted hordes from Genghis Khan to the British in 1920, and the Americans were no exception. The cries ranged from "Hello, thanks, and good-bye" to "Bring back Saddam." They had been horrified by the casualty toll taken by Rumsfeld's "humanitarian bombs": at least 5,400 civilians killed and countless others injured. Nor did it help that on board one of the first planes to arrive after the fall of Baghdad was the founder of the exiled Iraqi National Congress, Ahmad Chalabi, and a retinue of sixty. Chalabi was flown in by the neocons of the Office of Special Plans to plant their flag as a force in postwar governance. Although corrupt (he was wanted in Jordan for bank fraud), Chalabi was the Pentagon's golden boy. Even so, he was only faintly remembered by Iraqis as a wealthy self-promoter without a constituency.

When Iraq's WMD cupboard proved bare, leaving Bush looking like a loose cannon, he dodged accountability by curtly dismissing the whole affair as "revisionist history." At the same time, he didn't give up the search, tasking former arms inspector David Kay to gather a team and go over the country with a fine-tooth comb. From Bush's viewpoint, Kay was an ideal choice. As an NBC analyst, he had stubbornly clung to the notion that the two trailers were movable bioweapons labs. Five months later, however, Kay was forced to report to Congress that his 1,400-person Iraq Survey Group had found no evidence of a current WMD program. But Bush put a positive twist on the report, saying that preliminary findings of active research projects justified the war. On October 7, 2002, the president had declared, "Facing clear evidence of peril, we cannot wait for the final proof, the smoking gun which could come in the form of a mushroom cloud." Representative Ellen Tauscher, who had voted for the war based on Bush's WMD representations, scoffed at the overblown rhetoric. "Clearly, our administration puffed up, cherry picked and amplified—held on like a dog to a bone in its teeth—any piece of information they could that substantiated their predisposition to believing the worst," she said. "Now we find out not only that we may not have a smoking gun, we may not have a gun." Unfazed, Bush asked for $600 million to continue the scavenger hunt on top of the $300 million already spent.

Even the conservative columnist George Will thought that Bush should be held accountable for launching a preemptive strike on the basis of suspect evidence. "The doctrine of pre-emption—the core of the president's foreign policy—is in jeopardy," he wrote. Nor did Will let Bush off the hook on his ex post facto rationalization that humanitarian concerns were justification enough. "[U]nless one is prepared to postulate a U.S. right, perhaps even a duty," Will said, "to militarily dismantle any tyranny—on to Burma?—it is unacceptable to argue that Hussein's mass graves and torture chambers suffice as retrospective justification for a pre-emptive war." Will may not have known that, as revealed by Wolfowitz, the administration first decided on an invasion, then settled on a spurious WMD threat as an excuse.

When he boasted "Mission Accomplished" during his May Day flyboy act on the deck of the *Abraham Lincoln,* Bush elaborated: "The war on terrorism is not over, yet it is not endless. We do not know the day of final victory, but we have seen the turning of the tide." He was keeping up the pretense that the military campaign in Iraq was an integral part of the war on terror, but he soon learned that generals, bombers and tanks and, yes, aircraft carriers, are useless against al-Qaida and its affiliates. Twelve days after the carrier burlesque, al-Qaida pulled off a brilliantly planned bombing attack on a foreign residential compound in Riyadh, Saudi Arabia, that killed thirty-four, including nine Americans in the employ of defense contractor Vinnell Corporation. Al-Qaida released a chilling audiotape of radio transmissions between the attacking vehicles as they closed in on the compound that was played on *NBC News* on October 20, 2003. As a result of the Riyadh disaster, Bush was forced to downgrade his forecast: "This incident in Saudi Arabia shows that we still have a war to fight." That statement was scarcely uttered when suicide bombers hit an array of targets in Casablanca, taking forty-one lives.

When almost daily attacks on American troops in Iraq began and the death toll mounted, quickly exceeding the number killed in combat during the war proper, Bush, who schemed to keep himself out of harm's way during the Vietnam War, taunted, "Bring 'em on." This prompted the *San Francisco Chronicle* to describe the comment as "at best inappropriate — at worst insensitive to our troops and unduly provocative to our adversaries — considering that this country's mission is to calm the situation in 'postwar' Iraq." A wave of bombings hit, all with a message. On August 5, 2003, in a show of global reach, a suicide bomber attached to an Indonesian group allied with al-Qaida blasted the American-owned Marriott

Hotel in Jakarta, killing thirteen and wounding 139, including two Americans. Two days later a car bomb exploded at the Jordanian Embassy in Baghdad, leaving seventeen dead and one hundred injured; Jordan had dropped its support of the Saddam regime after Gulf War I and allowed U.S. troops to use its territory as a base. On August 19, the U.N. headquarters in a Baghdad hotel was the target of a bomb-laden cement truck, killing sixteen, among them a veteran U.N. diplomat. There followed a string of lethal attacks on people viewed as quislings, including policemen newly recruited by the Americans, a woman member of what was seen as a puppet government, and a moderate Muslim imam who urged cooperation with the occupiers. Bring 'em on, indeed.

Bush's verbal recklessness boomeranged. In October 2003, when he sought U.N. assistance in money and troops to bail him out of the mess he created by rejecting the advice of the world body, he initially ran into a wall of resistance. At home taxpayers and Congress sustained sticker shock at the price of the next year's budget to try to pacify and rebuild Iraq: $87 billion. And in Iraq the morale of U.S. troops had plunged. A poll taken by the military newspaper *Stars and Stripes* found that, in contradiction to the administration's rosy picture, fully one-third of the soldiers interviewed said that their morale was low to very low, citing long deployments in a dangerous mission that was not "clearly defined." (One GI had gone so far as to design a deck of playing cards depicting the most wanted men in the administration, topped by Bush, Cheney, Rumsfeld and Wolfowitz.) In what must have been a shocker to the commander in chief, 49 percent said it was "very likely" they would not reenlist once their hitches were up. And now Bush was running into a steelier Kofi Annan, the U.N. secretary-general, than when he was shoving the United Nations aside to go to war. Annan wanted the United

States to share power in setting up a government and writing a constitution, and concede to an early exit. Bush was forced to scale back his demands to get an agreement. At that it was mostly a symbolic victory since most member nations balked at writing a check and putting their own troops in harm's way. Bush's earlier disagreeability was undoubtedly on their minds.

The White House warriors liked to believe that Saddam Hussein loyalists gone underground were responsible for the violence, and that once he was killed or captured the threat would be gone. That was not a credible scenario. Opposition to the occupation was so widespread, according to reporters on the ground, that the demographics are hardly limited to Saddam's Ba'ath Party die-hards. Interviewed by the *San Francisco Chronicle*'s Anna Badkhen, Police Chief Riyad Abbas al Karbuli believed that there were tens of thousands of ordinary Iraqis fed up with an occupation that has left hundreds of innocent civilians dead. "It's true that the occupation changed the old regime," he said, "but if anyone occupied the United States by force, would you accept it? It is like a thorn. It keeps bothering you." At a wedding party near Baghdad, Badkhen found two dozen Iraqi equivalents of Joe Six-Pack dancing to a wailing kazoo as an older man, Mohammed Turki, proudly observed, "During the day we fight against the Americans. During the night we party like this." A religious note was struck by Sheikh Yunis Abdallah, an imam from Baqubah who had conspired against the Saddam regime. "Islam teaches us to fight wrong wherever you find it," he said. "So our people who fight against Americans have a right to do so." Badkhen found several youths fishing who had a different grievance against the occupation. "Before the war we had security," one of them, Mahmud, said. "Now we have thieves, looters and killers. This is what America brought." After a brief discussion, the group decided

that the only recourse was to kill Americans. The insurgency is growing, not abating. The word "quagmire" comes to mind.

To avoid further bloodshed, the prudent thing for Bush to do
would have been to pull out the troops and allow U.N. peacekeep-
ers to take over. But that meant ceding some control over the country, something he stubbornly resisted. He had gone to war not to
snuff out terrorism, of which Iraq was not guilty, but to gain the
geopolitical ends of his neocon cabal. An American occupation was
necessary to monopolize the Iraq oil industry.

So the war on terrorism had been in suspended animation as
Bush waged the campaign against Iraq. If al-Qaida had not been in
the country before, it was now. As Bush ruefully put it, Iraq has
become "a magnet for terrorists." Yet Bush continued to insist that
al-Qaida had been decimated, with half its high command either
killed or in custody. The Bali bombing in October 2002, which
claimed the lives of 202 foreign tourists, was traced to an indigenous
jihad unit, Jemaah Islamiyah, linked to al-Qaida. It occurred just as
Bush was focusing on the strike against Iraq, and should have signaled to him that his priorities were out of order. Sri Lankan terrorism expert Rohan Gunaratna, who analyzed thousands of recovered
al-Qaida documents, told *The New Yorker,* "I feel that if they had
not gone to Iraq they would have found Osama by now. The best
people were moved away from the operation. It's a great shame. It's
the biggest military failure in the war on terrorism so far." On August 11, 2003, *Time* magazine reported that government insiders believed that the change in emphasis allowed bin Laden to disperse to
other parts of the world operatives who survived the initial months
on the run. "The reason these guys were able to get away," a former
Bush official was quoted, "was because we let up." Dia'a Rashwan,
an expert on Islamic radicalism at Egypt's Al-Ahram Center for

Political and Strategic Studies, opined that Bush played into bin Laden's hands by invading Iraq. Bin Laden had claimed that the United States wanted to control Muslim lands, and the invasion was proof. Rashwan said that in the minds of many Muslims, "bin Laden said theoretical things, but now the theoretical things have become reality."

So a resurgent al-Qaida, energized by outrage in the Muslim world over the American conquest of Iraq, is upon us. It is just as Hosni Mubarak of Egypt prophesied: an unprovoked attack on Iraq would create millions of new Muslim radicals, a hundred new bin Ladens. A June 2003 Pew Research Center poll showed a dramatic decline in esteem for America since the war in key areas around the world, both Muslim and not. Eighty-three percent of Indonesians said they viewed the United States unfavorably, up from 60 percent a year earlier. Nearly 70 percent of those expressing negative views blamed Bush rather than the United States in general. In South Korea, only 46 percent of those queried held a positive view of the United States, down from 53 percent a year earlier. In Russia, only 36 percent said they had a favorable view of America, compared with 61 percent in 2002. Americans will find it more dangerous to live, travel and work abroad.

Although he had no aircraft carrier to land on, Osama bin Laden could claim victory in his personal battle with Bush. The president's kiss-off of him as "not important," after promising to "git" him, boomeranged in the aftermath of the invasion when the al-Qaida chieftain smuggled out audiotaped messages that were broadcast to the world by the al-Jazeera television outlet. One, on the second anniversary of 9/11, warned that new attacks would be coming around the globe. Another, on October 18, 2003, was even more ominous. Vowing suicide attacks "inside and outside" the United States, bin

Laden threatened: "We reserve the right to respond at the appropriate time and place against all the countries participating in this unjust war [against Iraq], particularly Britain, Spain, Australia, Poland, Japan and Italy," the latter five having sent token forces. Nor would the Islamic countries that joined in be spared, he said. Turning to the troops in Iraq, bin Laden declared: "Your blood will be spilled so the White House gang gets richer and the arms dealers with them, as well as the large companies involved." Mocking Bush's attempts to persuade other nations to send infantry to Iraq, bin Laden contended that Bush "thought that Iraq and its oil is a big treasure," but now has "resorted to buying mercenary fighters from East and West."

Mission not accomplished.

2

9/11

A few days after the 9/11 attacks, President George W. Bush stood on a pile of rubble at the site where the twin towers of the World Trade Center had stood, bullhorn in hand, flanked by New York City firemen, taking charge of the war on terror. The imagery of it all cast Bush as a decisive leader in a moment of national crisis, the defining moment of his neoteric presidency. The man who had lost the popular vote in the election ten months earlier and had to be saved by an ideology-driven Supreme Court saw himself catapulted overnight from an anemic 54 percent job approval rating into the stratosphere of the high 70s. Bush was the beneficiary of the tendency of Americans to rally around the president, whoever he may be, as a sign of unity against the enemy. There was an outpouring of symbolic patriotism—car aerials and even cereal boxes sprouted American flags. The dangerous habit of suspending critical faculties in critical times was in play.

On the morning of the 9/11 attacks, I arrived at the San Francisco International airport to catch a flight to France, only to find that air traffic was on an indefinite ground hold. For the next two days the Federal Aviation Administration kept all aircraft grounded, after which flights were severely restricted. Bill Clinton had to cancel a trip, while Al Gore was stranded in Austria. But it has recently come to light that there was a secret exception to the FAA's orders. Two days after 9/11, Prince Bandar bin Sultan, the veteran Saudi Arabian ambassador to Washington, sat down with President Bush in a meeting that had been scheduled prior to the attacks to discuss the Middle East peace process. Bandar, a smooth operator, had ready access to the White House through his role in obtaining Saudi financial help for the Nicaraguan Contras during the Reagan administration—he did a covert mission for Reagan's CIA director, William Casey— and his lengthy friendship with the first President Bush, who had personally profited from Saudi investment in his Carlyle Group, which cynics referred to as "recycled oil." But Bandar describes the relationship with both George Bushes as "like family." Indeed, it is so visceral he roots for the Dallas Cowboys football team.

Now, on September 13, the agenda had changed. For two days Bandar had been working the phones, talking with Colin Powell, with whom he had played racquetball at the Pentagon, and Condoleezza Rice, and now his Bush connections were paying off. As recounted in *Vanity Fair* for October 2003, "the day he met with the president, three Saudi men, all apparently in their 20s, were escorted to a private hangar in Tampa, where they boarded an eight-passenger Learjet and took off for Blue Grass Airport in Lexington, Kentucky. There they were greeted by an American who helped them with their baggage as they made their way onto a waiting Boeing 747 with Arabic writing on it, which then, presumably, took off for parts unknown." Over the next few days, the magazine reported, planes around the country shuttled members of the House of Saud, influential Saudis and members of the bin Laden family, of which Osama was the black sheep, to East Coast airports for flights home. By the third week in September, the Bandar airlift had spirited some 140 Saudis, among them at least 11 bin Ladens, out of the United States.

As it turned out, fifteen of the nineteen 9/11 hijackers were Saudi nationals, and Osama bin Laden was wanted for the American embassy bombing in Kenya in August 1998. Yet the FBI made no move to interview the fleeing Saudis, and in fact denied—as did the FAA—that there had been an airlift. The agencies' denials were contradicted by Richard Clarke, head of the Counterterrorism Security Group of the National Security Council at the time. Clarke, who served under Clinton as well as George W. Bush and is famously independent, told *Vanity Fair* that immediately after 9/11 he was approached by someone in the Situation Room, a bunkerlike underground suite in the West Wing, about repatriating the Saudis. "Somebody brought to us for approval the decision to let an airplane filled with Saudis, including members of the bin Laden family, leave the country," Clarke said. "My role was to say that it can't happen until the FBI approves it. And so the FBI was asked—we had a live connection to the FBI—and we asked the FBI to make sure that they were satisfied that everybody getting on that plane was someone that was OK to leave. And they came back and said, yes, it was fine with them. So we said, 'Fine, let it happen.'"

Everybody OK to leave? Four thousand relatives of the 9/11 victims have filed a $1 trillion civil action in Washington charging members of the royal House of Saud and the bin Laden family—whose huge Saudi Binladen Group construction firm won contracts from the royals to restore the mosque-shrines in Mecca and Medina, strongholds of the fiery Wahhabi sect that has been a spawning ground for terrorists—and scores of others with wrongful death, conspiracy and racketeering. The heart of the lawsuit is that they knew or should have known that certain Islamic charities to which they contributed sizable funds were actually al-Qaida fronts. Prominent attorney Allan Gerson, co-lead counsel for the plaintiffs, believes the FBI should have questioned the bin Ladens and members of the House of Saud before they were allowed to leave the country. The line of questioning: "What did they know about the financing of al-Qaida? What did they know about the use of charitable institutions in the United States and elsewhere as conduits for terrorism financing? Why was the Saudi government not responsive to Clinton administration pleas in 1999 and 2000 that they stop turning a blind eye to terrorist financing through Saudi banks and charities?"

Those questions may never be asked of the defendants, since most are now beyond the reach of U.S. law. Of the Clinton initiative, Richard Clarke said that some of the Saudi mucketymucks "were clearly sympathetic to al-Qaida, some of them thought that if they allowed a certain degree of cooperation with al-Qaida, al-Qaida would leave them alone. And some of them were merely acting in a knee-jerk, instinctive way to what was believed to be interference in their internal affairs."

It now seems clear that Bush began losing the war on terrorism on day one when he authorized the Saudi exodus, for it turned out that there were a few royals and bin Ladens who were in a position to furnish information on al-Qaida or were suspected of channeling funds, wittingly or unwittingly, to it. Osama bin Laden founded the terrorist organization in the late 1980s with millions of dollars received from his family's Saudi Binladen Group construction fortune. Osama was not the lone bin Laden involved in Islamic militancy during this period. His older half brother, Mahrous, was implicated with the Muslim Brotherhood in what was known as the Mecca Affair, a 1979 insurrection against the House of Saud that caused more than one hundred deaths.

Although the FBI had no blanket investigation of influential Saudis residing in the United States at the time of 9/11, in 1996 it had opened a file on two other siblings, Abdullah and Omar bin Laden, who were tied in with the American branch of the World Assembly of Muslim Youth (WAMY). As reported in the British periodical *The Guardian*, the Bureau's file showed that WAMY, which fronts as a charity, was cited by Indian officials and the Philippine military for supporting terrorism in their countries. On September 19, 2001, when the Saudi evacuation project remained under way, the FBI reopened its file on Abdullah and Omar. According to David Armstrong, an investigator for the Public Education Center, which examined the FBI file, "These documents show there was an open FBI investigation into these guys at the time of their departure."

Shortly after 9/11, Carmen bin Laden, an estranged sister-in-law of Osama's, volunteered to *ABC News* that some family members may have donated money to al-Qaida. And according to *Vanity Fair*, "Osama's brother-in-law Mohammed Jamal Khalifa was widely reported to be an important figure in al-Qaeda and was accused of having ties to the 1993 World Trade Center bombing, to the October 2000 bombing of the U.S.S. Cole, and to the funding of a Philippine terrorist group." Khalil bin Laden, who was evacuated from Orlando, Florida, had caught the eye of Brazilian authorities monitoring suspected terrorist training activity in a remote section of Minas Gerais state, home to a large population of Islamic expatriates. According to the Brazilian newspaper *O Globo*, Khalil had suspicious "business" connections in the area, which some call the Terrorist Triangle.

It is a matter of high irony that Prince Bandar himself has not gone unsullied by the 9/11 blowback. His father, Defense Minister Prince Sultan, who has an American air base named after him, is a named defendant in the lawsuit filed by the 9/11 victims' families. Since 1994, Sultan contributed at least $6 million to four charities that subsidized Osama bin Laden and al-Qaida. His own attorneys concede that for sixteen consecutive years he made annual payments of some $266,000 to the Saudi Arabia–based International Islamic Relief Organization (IIRO). According to the lawsuit's bill of particulars, the IIRO funnels laundered monies to al-Qaida and its affiliates and acts as a recruiting and training center for some. It alleges that the IIRO was involved with the 1993 World Trade Center truck bombing, the plot to destroy the Lincoln Tunnel and Brooklyn Bridge, the conspiracy to assassinate President Bill Clinton and Pope John Paul II, a grand scheme to simultaneously blow up twelve American airliners in Asian skies, and the 1998 embassy bombings in Kenya and Tanzania.

The IIRO spider's web is worldwide. Osama's brother-in-law, Mohammed Khalifa, headed the Philippine branch that collected and laundered money for operations in the region, which are carried out by two al-Qaida units, the Moro Islamic Liberation Front and the Abu Sayyaf Group, both noted for their kidnappings of American and European travelers. A former Abu Sayyaf member disclosed: "Less than 30 percent of the IIRO funds went to legitimate public works, the rest going toward the purchase of weapons." According to Canadian intelligence documents, Mohmous Jaballah, who belonged to the Egyptian al-Jihad led by Osama bin Laden's second in command, Ayman al-Zawahiri, and was tried in Canada, was an employee of the IIRO. Arafat el-Ashi, the IIRO's man in Canada, testified at the Jaballah trial that the IIRO and its parent,

the Muslim World League, were intimately connected to and subsidized by certain Saudi Arabian interests. He made it clear that as
an employee of the IIRO and the Muslim World League he was
also an employee of the Saudi government. The IIRO's secretary-
general, Adnan Basha, was more specific when he wrote: "The major finance is coming from the generous people of Saudi Arabia,
King Fahd, and the royal family."

Through an attorney, Prince Sultan acknowledged that he had
authorized the annual grants to the IIRO as part of his official duties, and did not wittingly fund terrorism. But this doesn't answer
the question of why a defense minister would be writing checks to
charities, or whether the Saudi intelligence services are so inept
they didn't know about the flip side of the IIRO.

The wife of Prince Bandar, Princess Haifa al-Faisal, a daughter
of the late King Faisal, also was swept into the controversy when in
its November 22, 2002, issue *Newsweek* revealed that money she gave,
$130,000 in all, purportedly for an operation needed by a Saudi
woman in San Diego, was funneled through cutouts to two of the
9/11 hijackers, Khalid al-Midhar and Nawaf Alhazmi, while they
were marking time in San Diego before plunging an airliner into
the Pentagon. The two cutouts, Omar al-Bayoumi and Osama
Basnan, were vocal admirers of Osama bin Laden, with Basnan cel-
ebrating 9/11 as a "wonderful, glorious day." It was learned that al-
Bayoumi paid $1,500 to cover the first two months' rent for an
apartment next door to his own for the two hijackers when they first
arrived from Malaysia, while Basnan was married to the woman
who was said to have needed the surgery, Majida Ibrahim. On December 9, 2002, the *Weekly Standard* commented that "those who
have followed the activities of Islamic terrorist charities also recognize an interesting fact about al-Midhar and Alhazmi, the hijacker

recipients of the princess's largesse. These men were not mere foot soldiers in the conspiracy. They are the same two men who were tracked by Malaysian intelligence and the CIA after their attendance at an al-Qaida planning meeting in Kuala Lumpur in 2000, as they traveled across the Pacific and into this country—where their trail went cold thanks to bureaucratic infighting between the CIA and FBI. They were big fish—perhaps among the biggest in the team." It might be added that the CIA eventually informed the FBI that al-Midhar and Alhazmi were in the country. But by that time—three weeks before 9/11—it was too late. Bureau agents vainly chased their tails, not even alerting their informants.

Princess Haifa tearfully told the media that she had no idea how the compassionate donation she had made wound up in the bank account of the wife of a man who had helped the pair of hijackers. "I felt the whole world fell on my head," she said. The Saudi Embassy mounted a public relations blitz portraying the princess as a victim as well; she received a consoling call from Laura Bush, and was widely seen as blameless. But the point was missed. "Prince Bandar and Princess Haifa know that the Wahhabi religious hierarchy in Saudi Arabia preaches hatred and contempt of Christians, Jews, traditional Muslims, Shiites, Hindus, and Sikhs," the *Weekly Standard* observed. "They know that the same religious hierarchy has operated Islamic outreach and charitable institutions like the Muslim World League, the World Assembly of Muslim Youth, and the International Islamic Relief Organization (all with offices in the U.S.) that have served as cover for terrorism. They know that financial gifts or donations to these bodies or their hangers-on are likely to end up in the hands of the terrorists."

It appears that President Bush's green light for Bandar to evacuate the royals and bin Ladens in the immediate wake of 9/11 was no more than a continuation of his protecting them from investigation before the attacks. *The Guardian* of London reported on November 7, 2001, that

> FBI and military intelligence officials in Washington say they were prevented for political reasons from carrying out full investigations into members of the Bin Laden family in the U.S. before the terrorist attacks of September 11. U.S. intelligence agencies have come under criticism for their wholesale failure to predict the catastrophe at the World Trade Centre. But some are complaining that their hands were tied. FBI documents shown on BBC Newsnight last night and obtained by the Guardian show that they had earlier sought to investigate two of Osama bin Laden's relatives in Washington and a Muslim organization, the World Assembly of Muslim Youth (WAMY), with which they were linked.

The article pointed out that Abdullah bin Laden, who was the U.S. director of WAMY, and his sibling Omar, who resided in suburban Virginia, were the targets of the aborted FBI probe. It closed by saying: "High-placed intelligence sources in Washington told the Guardian this week: 'There were always constraints on investigating the Saudis.' They said the restrictions became worse after the Bush administration took over this year. The intelligence agencies had been told to 'back off' from investigations involving other members of the bin Laden family, the Saudi royals, and possible Saudi links to the acquisition of nuclear weapons by Pakistan. 'There were particular investigations that were effectively killed.'"

The freeze on investigating Saudis was confirmed by a bevy of conscience-stricken FBI agents who came forth following 9/11. A New York agent, testifying behind a screen to shield him from re-crimination, told the Joint House-Senate Intelligence Committee looking into missed signals that allowed the attacks to happen that he warned his superiors "someone would die" if the trail of Khalid al-Midhar was not more actively pursued. Al-Midhar of course was the hijacker in San Diego—his name and phone number were listed in the local directory—to whom charitable money from Princess Haifa was channeled. Attorney General John Ashcroft was enraged not at the egregious lapse but at the agent for disclosing it. In July 2003, an Arab-American agent named Bassem Youssef filed a lawsuit claiming that the FBI, among other misdeeds, deliberately missed the boat in collecting intelligence on Osama bin Laden. He cited a case in which, two months before 9/11, a "walk-in" at one of the Bureau field offices offered to divulge significant information about the al-Qaida commander. The field office requested that Youssef debrief the potential informant because of his expertise and language skills—the FBI had only a handful of Arabic speakers. But Youssef was not given the go-ahead, and the man left, taking with him whatever data he might have possessed.

Another example of the FBI sticking its head in the sand came with the revelations of veteran agents Robert G. Wright Jr. of the Chicago division's Terrorism Task Force and his partner, John Vincent. As told on *ABC News Primetime Live* on December 19, 2002, the story began in 1996 when the pair was assigned, with growing terrorism in the Middle East as a backdrop, "to track a connection to Chicago, a suspected terrorist cell that would later lead them to an Osama bin Laden connection." But Wright and Vincent discovered that all the headquarters International Terrorism Unit wanted them to do was follow the suspected terrorists around town and file reports, but make no arrests. Then in 1998 came the twin U.S. Embassy bombings in East Africa, claiming some two hundred lives. Wright and Vincent recounted that some of the money for those attacks "led back to the people they had been tracking in Chicago, and to a powerful Saudi Arabian businessman—this man,

Yassin Kadi [photo on screen], who had extensive business and financial ties in Chicago." Still, headquarters ordered no arrests. Former federal prosecutor Mark Flessner confirmed that Wright and Vincent were helping him build a strong indictment of Kadi and others when they were shut down. "There were powers bigger than I was in the Justice Department and within the FBI that simply were not going to let it happen," Flessner asserted. "And it didn't happen."

The ABC program's announcer, Brian Ross, gave the bottom line: "On September the 11th, the two agents watched in horror, worried that the men they could have stopped years earlier were involved. And now, the White House says they were. One month after the attacks, the U.S. government officially identified Yassin Al Kadi as one of Osama bin Laden's important financiers, a specially designated global terrorist, the same man who, years earlier, the FBI had ordered agents Vincent and Wright to leave alone."

From his office in Riyadh, Kadi told Ross: "Not one cent went to Osama bin Laden." He didn't say to whom it went.

Emotionally labeling the FBI's International Terrorism Unit a "spectator" while Americans died on 9/11, Robert Wright completed a 500-page manuscript entitled *Fatal Betrayals of the Intelligence Mission* shortly after the attacks and submitted it to FBI Director Robert Mueller as internal rules require (after this author, a former agent, published *Hoover's FBI* in 1970, agents were required to sign a secrecy agreement allowing the Bureau to censor all publications). In an unusual move, Mueller sealed all of it, going so far as to block the Joint House-Senate Intelligence Committee from receiving a copy and threatening Wright with criminal prosecution. In point of fact, Mueller's own actions might be considered obstruction of justice.

So might the White House decision to make an exception to the aviation restrictions in the wake of 9/11 at the urgent bidding of Prince Bandar. Boston's Logan International airport, from where the two hijacked planes departed that crashed into the World Trade Center, was particularly slow to get back to normal due to security issues. So when a call came into Logan's Emergency Operations Center on September 19, Director of Aviation Tom Kinton was appalled. At the time President Bush's speechwriters were putting the finishing touches on a somber address delivered the next day. "Our war on terrorism . . . will not end until every terrorist group of global reach has been found, stopped and defeated," Bush perorated. The call instructed Kinton that a plane that had originated in Los Angeles and made stops in Orlando and Dulles airports to pick up members of the bin Laden family was to be allowed to land at Logan, where eleven more bin Ladens would board. Kinton and his staff were ordered to then clear the plane for takeoff for Saudi Arabia. "We were in the midst of the worst terrorist act in history," Kinton marveled, "and here we were seeing an evacuation of the bin Ladens!"

3

OIL SLICK

In retrospect it seems unbelievable that in the frantic hours after the 9/11 attacks, when it was uncertain whether further attacks were coming, George W. Bush didn't cancel a White House meeting scheduled with Prince Bandar two days after the attacks and turn down his request for the special privilege of permitting the repatriation of Saudi royals and bin Laden family members when all other civilian aircraft were forbidden to fly. Although there was no suggestion the president knew that the FBI had an open file on two bin Laden brothers in the United States, or that Bandar's wife had contributed indirectly to two of the hijackers, lifting the ban for them and asking the FBI to expedite their premature evacuation instead of questioning them was a serious breach of national security.

That Bush didn't seem to even think twice about what he was doing is mute testimony to the entangling alliances between the Bush family, the Saudi business oligarchs such as the bin Ladens, and the Saudi royal family, intertwined relationships that are both personal and financial. One can look at it and simply say that what

Bush did was an automatic quid pro quo for the Saudis' investment in the senior Bush's Carlyle Group, a $12 billion private equity firm with heavy holdings in defense contractors' stocks. As former *Time* reporter Nina Burleigh put it, "The Carlyle connection means that George Bush senior is on the payroll of private interests that have defense business before the government while his son is president." Charles Lewis of the Center for Public Integrity was even more explicit in saying that "in a really peculiar way, George W. Bush could, some day, benefit financially from his own administration's decisions, through his father's investments."

The first President Bush began to exploit his special relationship with the Saudi power structure shortly after he had done them the favor of launching Operation Desert Storm in 1991 to oust Iraqi forces from Kuwait. Why Saddam Hussein invaded the corrupt little kingdom to begin with is a matter of some conjecture, as it held no threat to him. During the 1980s the Reagan-Bush administration tilted toward Iraq in its protracted war with Iran, which had held Americans hostage. Hussein became a trading partner of the United States, receiving loans, arms, food, military intelligence and moral support. When the Iraqis overran Kuwait, there was some talk that the U.S. ambassador to Baghdad, April Glaspie, had unintentionally conveyed to Hussein the idea that he should invade Kuwait in a conversation shortly beforehand. According to an article by Helga Graham in *The London Observer* captioned "U.S. Oil Plot Fueled Saddam," the United States did everything it could to push Hussein into Kuwait, holding a secret meeting in New York urging Iraq to engineer a big oil price rise. "[Secretary of State] James Baker was attempting to have a State Department human rights report critical of Saddam's regime suppressed. Huge credits to Iraq were continued despite sanctions waived by the president [Bush]." The upshot of the invasion was a surge in world oil prices such as ordinarily happens when there is regional instability. The beneficiaries, of course, are the oil-producing countries and the petroleum cartels. But the Saudis feared that Hussein might not stop at Kuwait, and welcomed the U.S. intervention.

Returning to the private sector after his defeat by Bill Clinton in 1992, Bush as well as his erstwhile secretary of state, the taciturn, trusted James A. Baker, moved to capitalize on the Saudi affinity. Baker became senior counselor of the Carlyle Group, then Bush signed on as senior adviser. They were in effect setup men for the sales pitch, making several trips to Saudi Arabia with Carlyle executives in tow to meet with the royals and wealthy businessmen. Carlyle's CEO, David Rubenstein, told *Vanity Fair's* Craig Unger how it worked, which wasn't exactly like a Tupperware party. As a world mover and shaker, Bush would not be so crass as to give a sales talk himself. "Bush's speeches are about what it's like to be a former president, and what it's like to be the father of a president," Rubenstein explained. "He doesn't talk about Carlyle or solicit investors." After the speeches, Rubenstein and his fund-raising team would come in for the money. According to the *Washington Post*, Prince Bandar was among those who invested, and in 1995 the bin Ladens came aboard. Joining them were the bin Mahfouzes, Saudi Arabia's largest banking family, whose patriarch is billionaire Khalid bin Mahfouz, whose sister was married to Osama bin Laden. Mahfouz founded the National Commercial Bank, through which, according to U.S. intelligence officials quoted by *Scoop* on August 28, 2002, he and others transferred "tens of millions of dollars to bank accounts linked to indicted terrorist Osama bin Laden." His sons, Abdul Rahman and Sultan, became Carlyle investors as well. It is of more than passing interest that Abdul Rahman bin Mahfouz was a director of the Muwafaq Foundation, designated by the U.S. Treasury Department as "an al-Qaida front." The attorney for Abdul Rahman and Sultan, Cherif Sedky, told Unger that the brothers "made an investment in one of the Carlyle funds in 1995 which is in the neighborhood of $30 million." Sedky stated that the bin Mahfouz family renounces terrorism and denied that monies they donated to charities have been used to finance terrorists.

The we-are-family cachet between the Bushes and Saudis dates back to the early 1980s, when George H. W. Bush was Reagan's vice president and Prince Bandar was a Saudi diplomatic officer newly arrived in Washington. In cultivating highly placed officials, Bandar found easy access to the veep, who was not regarded as a heavyweight. Bush soon found out that Saudi Arabia was a potential golden money spigot. Although the desert kingdom had no vital national interest in the struggle in Nicaragua at the time between the leftist Sandinista government and the Contras, Bandar arranged for millions of dollars to be contributed to the rebels in contravention of the Boland Act in Congress, which forbade U.S. aid. After Watergate, Bush had been President Gerald Ford's second choice as CIA director (the first choice was celebrated attorney Edward Bennett Williams, who didn't want to give up his beloved Washington Redskins football team); in the post Bush signed off internal memos as "chief spook." The Saudi funds of course had to be run through CIA clandestine channels, so Bandar himself became a spook of sorts in working with the Agency.

At the same time, with the Middle East in turmoil, the United States helped the Saudis in a gigantic buildup of airfields, ports and military bases, with the lion's share of the contracts going to the Saudi Binladen Group. Americans trained and armed troops for Afghanistan to combat the Soviet occupiers. The two countries spent some $40 billion recruiting, supplying and training nearly 100,000 militant mujahedeen from forty Muslim countries, including Saudi Arabia, Pakistan, Iran, Algeria and Afghanistan itself. Among those recruited were Osama bin Laden and his cadres. According to Laura Secor in the *Boston Globe* on December 15, 2002, the messianic bin Laden imported engineers and equipment from his family's Saudi Binladen Group to construct tunnels for guerrilla training centers and hospitals, and for arms dumps near the Pakistan frontier. After the Soviets withdrew from Afghanistan, the CIA and the Pakistani intelligence unit ISI sponsored the Taliban, a regime composed of the fanatic Wahhabi sect, the same sect that is the state religion of Saudi Arabia. The Wahhabi Taliban had the nod of the House of Saud as well as the bin Laden and Mahfouz clans, Saudi Arabia's superrich.

(Ironically, the infrastructure set up in the name of anticommunism has been now converted into a shelter and base for the most notorious Islamic terrorism organization, al-Qaida. The CIA tried to buy back the thousands of Stinger shoulder-fired, surface-to-air missiles it distributed to yesterday's anti-Soviet fighters, but it was no sale. These weapons and others in the arsenal are now being deployed against American forces.)

The name that drags George W. Bush into this web of intrigue is, surprisingly, not the dashing Prince Bandar but a behind-the-scenes operator, James R. Bath. They met in the Texas Air National Guard and became fast buddies. Nominally an aircraft broker, Bath broke into the financial big time in 1976 when, according to the *Houston Chronicle*'s Pete Brewton, "Bath was named a trustee for Sheikh Salem bin Laden of Saudi Arabia [half-brother of Osama bin Laden].
. . . Bath's job was to handle all of bin Laden's North American investments and operations." Shortly thereafter Bath landed the

account of Khalid bin Mahfouz, the megabanker who would later invest in the Carlyle Group. In 1979, Bath invested $50,000 in George W. Bush's foundering Arbusto Energy for a 5 percent share. Because it was not prudent as an investment, it appears to have been more a donation to Bush personally as a member of an upwardly mobile political family. Skeptics alleged that the money wasn't out of Bath's pocket but originated with bin Laden and bin Mahfouz. Journalist Wayne Madsen in "Questionable Ties: Tracking bin Laden's money flow leads back to Midland, Texas," stated: "In conflicting statements, Bush at first denied ever knowing Bath, then acknowledged his stake in Arbusto and that he was aware Bath represented Saudi interests."

Young Bush went on to parlay his Arbusto holding into a fortune, aided by friendly bailouts along the line. In September 1984, William DeWitt and Mercer Reynolds, owners of a small petroleum enterprise called Spectrum 7 Energy, purchased Arbusto. As part of the deal, Bush was named president and received a 13.6 percent equity. According to *U.S. News & World Report*, March 16, 1992, oil prices stayed low, and within two years Spectrum was in trouble. At this point Spectrum was bought out by the larger Harken Energy Corporation in what only can be described as a sweetheart deal. In the six months before the acquisition, the magazine reported, Spectrum had lost $400,000. But Harken tendered Bush and his partners more than $2 million in stock in the 180-well operation. Made a director and hired as a "consultant," Bush was given another $600,000 in stock and a cushy salary.

As it turned out, the Harken corporate officers knew what they were doing. In 1987, as the company began to struggle, James Bath's client, the ubiquitous Khalid bin Mahfouz, came to the rescue. Bin Mahfouz had set up a small Houston bank to process investment transactions. Tom Flocco in *Scoop* for August 28, 2002, disclosed that Khalid used the bank as a funnel for Saudi financier Abdullah Bakhsh to buy 17 percent of Harken's stock, providing a cash infusion of $25 million. As a result, Bakhsh's American associate, Talet Othman, was given a seat on the board of directors with Bush. According to the *Wall Street Journal*, Othman also had a seat at the elder Bush's White House foreign policy table, having become a Saudi agent of influence. "[S]ince August 1990, the Palestinian-born Chicago investor has attended three White House meetings with President Bush to discuss Middle East policy," the *Journal* said.

Then, in January 1990, Harken was awarded a contract by Bahrain, Saudi Arabia's neighbor in the Persian Gulf, giving it the exclusive offshore drilling rights for oil and gas. If oil and gas were discovered, Harken would have sole transportation and marketing rights. "This is an incredible deal, unbelievable for this small company," energy analyst Charles Strain told *Forbes*, the business magazine. What Swain didn't note was that the son of the president of the United States was on Harken's board—if he had, he wouldn't have been so incredulous. Lacking sufficient capital to explore off the Bahrain coast, Harken partnered with Bass Enterprises Production Company of Fort Worth. The Bass brothers contributed more than $200,000 to the Republican Party during the late 1980s and early 1990s.

On June 22, 1990, George W. Bush sold his Harken stock for a cool 200 percent profit. One week after the sale, the company announced a $23.2 million quarterly earnings loss, and the stock price plummeted 60 percent over the next six months. "There is substantial evidence to suggest that Bush knew Harken was in dire straits in the weeks before he sold the $848,560 of Harken stock," *U.S. News & World Report* observed in its issue of March 16, 1992. He was on a "fairness committee" to study possible restructuring of the company, and on the audit committee vetting the books with the accountancy firm Arthur Andersen. He violated SEC regulations by not promptly reporting insider stock deals, which was due by July 10, 1990. In fact, he missed by a mile, not filing the report until March 1991. His tardiness triggered an SEC probe, which ruled that he was in violation but recommended no criminal prosecution. It was a glaring case of presidential son immunity. Household maven Martha Stewart, now criminally charged with a similar offense, should be so lucky.

What may help explain George W. Bush's post-9/11 reluctance to shake up the CIA is the depth of the Agency's penetration into the Bushes' business affairs. The resident agent for Khalid bin Mahfouz and Salem bin Laden, James Bath, had a close business partner named Charles W. "Bill" White, with whom he had a number of profitable land development deals. A decorated fighter pilot, White played the point man in the deals while Bath stage-managed from the wings. White divulged to *Time* reporters Jonathan Beaty and S. C. Gwynne: "Bath told me that he was in the CIA. He told me he was recruited by George H. W. Bush himself in 1976." White added, "That made sense to me, especially in light of what I had seen once we went into business together. He [Bath] said that Bush wanted him involved with the Arabs, and to get into the aviation business." White revealed that Bath developed a network of offshore companies to camouflage the movement of money and aircraft between Texas and the Middle East, primarily Saudi Arabia. One, affiliated with Harken, was in the Cayman Islands.

In 1992 Khalid bin Mahfouz was indicted in New York on charges that he had schemed to defraud depositors, regulators and auditors of the insolvent Bank of Credit and Commerce International (BCCI), one of the rankest frauds ever. As characterized by J. H.

Hatfield in his volume *Fortunate Son*, "A deal broker [James Bath] whose alleged associations run from the CIA to a major shareholder and director of the Bank of Credit and Commerce International. BCCI was closed down in July 1991 amid charges of multi-billion dollar frauds and worldwide news reports that the institution had been involved in covert intelligence work, drug money laundering, arms brokering, bribery of government officials, and aid to terrorists." In their work, Beaty and Gwynne give a witness's description:

> Sami Masri began talking again, the hushed words tumbling out, painting a detailed, vivid description of the Bank of Credit and Commerce International's global involvement with drug shipments, smuggled gold, stolen military secrets, assassinations, bribery, extortion, covert intelligence operations, and weapons deals. These were the province of a Karachi-based (Pakistan) cadre of bank operatives, paramilitary units, spies, and enforcers who handled BCCI's darkest operations around the globe and trafficked in bribery and corruption.

In view of the Pakistan connection, it is possible that Osama bin Laden bought weapons through the BCCI cover for his budding al-Qaida.

According to a *Wall Street Journal* story on December 6, 1991, a Harken investor, the real estate heavy-hitter Abdullah Bakhsh, was a financial partner in Saudi Arabia with Ghaith Pharaon, identified by the U.S. Federal Reserve Board as a "front man" for BCCI's secret acquisition of U.S. banks. Pharaon was an intriguing figure in the scandal. As Saudi Arabia's intelligence director during the 1970s, he met and became friends with his CIA counterpart, George H. W. Bush. After both left their intelligence posts, they continued to do business together. In his book *The Conspirators*, Al Martin alleged that in the mid-1980s Gulf Oil Drilling Supply of Miami, New York and Bahrain was Jeb Bush's vehicle for fraud. "The fraud was rather simple," Martin wrote. "Richard Secord [the retired general who would figure prominently in the Iran-Contra affair] arranged through then Vice President George Bush's old friend, Ghaith Pharaon, the then retired head of Saudi intelligence, for Gulf Oil Drilling Supply to purchase from the Saudi government oil and gas leases in the Persian Gulf which were effectively worthless." The leases would be dressed up to look extremely valuable, then used as loan collateral. The Great American Bank & Trust of West Palm Beach subsequently collapsed under the weight of unpaid loans.

The interlock between the Bushes and unsavory Saudis is further illustrated by the BCCI affair. Ghaith Pharaon, who represented BCCI, was the chief stockholder in a Houston bank of which James Bath was a part owner. With branches in seventy-three countries, BCCI proceeded, according to the *Boston Herald* on December 11, 2001, to defraud depositors of $10 billion during the 1980s, while providing a money laundry used by the Medellin drug cartel, Asia's major narcotics consortiums, Manuel Noriega, Saddam Hussein, the CIA and Islamic terrorist organizations worldwide.

Senators Bob Graham and Richard C. Shelby, leaders of the joint Senate-House panel that investigated the 9/11 attacks, called on the Bush administration to declassify information concerning Saudi funding of terrorists. Shelby argued: "I believe [the Saudis] cannot support so-called charities that support terrorism on a big scale, and then pretend that they're our friends or our allies. As we get into the money trail, it might be embarrassing, but the American people need to know; the victims and their families need to know." Graham asked a rhetorical question: "Will we get [the information declassified] in thirty years when the archives are open, or will we get it in time, before the next attack?"

But George W. Bush turned a deaf ear to the appeal for transparency, while his long-term symbiosis with the Saudis remained intact. He entertained Crown Prince Abdullah at his Crawford, Texas, ranch, a site he reserves for the specially privileged. A few months later Prince Bandar and Princess Haifa received a royal welcome at the spread. George H. W. Bush continued to be Bandar's guest at his palatial Aspen resort home, and flew off with the prince in his private Airbus to go bird hunting in Spain. The relationship is so intimate that the prince has been called Bandar Bush.

It is as if nothing had happened.

4

TROPICAL TERRORISM

In May 2002, George W. Bush delivered a fist-pounding ritual denunciation of Fidel Castro in Miami before the wildly receptive audience of the Cuban Liberty Council, the most rabid of the anti-Castro exile groupings in South Florida. Sitting in the audience as guest of honor was a scowling man with horn-rimmed glasses named Orlando Bosch, a lapsed pediatrician who was an icon among the radical exiles for his long career as an international terrorist. He could fairly be called the Osama bin Laden of the anti-Castro cause. The tour de force of Dr. Death, as he had come to be called, was the 1976 midair bombing of a Cuban airliner that took the lives of all seventy-three people on board. But in the same year he had also conspired to assassinate by bombing former Secretary of State Henry Kissinger, whom he viewed as too soft on Castro, during a visit to Costa Rica; the plot was aborted when local authorities, acting on a tip, arrested Bosch. After Bosch reentered the United States illegally in 1989, the Justice Department, citing an FBI report that he "repeatedly expressed and demonstrated a willingness to cause indiscriminate injury and death," had ruled that he should be deported. But along came a champion of his cause, Jeb Bush, then a budding Florida politician, who interceded with his father, the president. The ruling was overturned.

It was arranged that Bosch be seated in the front row for the Cuban Liberty Council event, reported Roger Gathman in the *San Francisco Chronicle,* December 1, 2002, for one of those grinning photo ops that President Bush so craves. But at the last moment Bush's handlers realized that having him press the flesh with a notorious terrorist might not play well in the rest of the country in the post-9/11 climate. Bosch was hustled to a middle row, where he became just another face in the crowd.

The incident hints at the deep affinity, born of political opportunism, of the Bush family toward the Cuban expatriates in Florida, and shows their hypocrisy when it comes to terrorism. The bloc consists of some 800,000 ethnic Cubans of varying shades of hostility to the Castro regime, a number that looms big come election time in the state. Indeed, Jeb Bush delivered the majority of the Cuban vote to his brother in Campaign 2000, which made the election so close as to allow the Supreme Court to step in and abort a recount. The gravitational pull between the Bushes and shady power brokers in the Cuban community traces back to the 1970s, when the elder Bush was CIA director. As investigative journalist Jack Colhoun put it in the Summer 1992 *Covert Action Quarterly*:

> George Herbert Walker Bush is the first former CIA director to serve as president. The implications for U.S. policy of Bush's move from CIA headquarters to the White House were profound and chilling, but seldom the subject of mainstream political discussion. . . . The Bushes' shadowy business partners come straight out of the world in which the CIA thrives—the netherworld of secret wars and covert operations, drug runners,

mafiosi, and crooked entrepreneurs out to make a fast buck. . . .
In return for throwing business their way, the Bushes give their
partners political access, legitimacy, and perhaps protection.
The big loser in the deal is the democratic process.

It sounds like Saudi déjà vu all over again. And it is.

For George W. Bush, the overwhelming urge for regime change
in Havana was in the genes. As CIA director, his father had personally gone to extreme lengths to protect the exile bigwigs plotting
against Castro after the 1976 Washington car bombing that killed
former Chilean diplomat Orlando Letelier—an opponent of the
brutal regime of General Augusto Pinochet—and an aide, Ronni
Moffitt. At first Bush's CIA planted stories that Pinochet's secret
police, DINA, was not culpable, then depicted Letelier as a Castro
agent. When the FBI determined that DINA had in fact master-
minded the murders, dispatching CIA-trained Cuban exiles from
Miami as the actual assassins, Bush showed up in the Little Havana
section of Miami under the guise of a "walking tour." According to
Donald Freed and Fred Landis in their book *Death in Washington*,
Bush met secretly with FBI Special Agent in Charge Julius Matson
(under whom I had served in Seattle) and his counterterrorism supervisor, admonishing them not to allow their probe to rise above
the lowest-level Cubans. In the end, three known exile terrorists,
who years earlier had fired a bazooka at the U.N. building in New
York, were convicted. An American DINA agent who was a CIA
asset, Michael Vernon Townley, was permitted to plead guilty to
greatly reduced charges. No one of higher status was ever charged,
and any CIA role went unexplored.

In the mid-1980s the ex-CIA director and Jeb Bush became the
Republican Party's unofficial ambassadors to the Cuban-American
colony in the Miami area. They did not scruple to support even the

most corrupt, immoral and extreme of the lot for their own gain. The case of Miguel Recarey Jr. makes the point. Recarey came from a wealthy, politically connected Havana family whose uncle had been minister of health under Fulgencio Batista, the venal dictator Castro ousted. Once in Florida, Recarey did business with organized crime, becoming a familiar figure to law enforcement officers monitoring the gangsters. The *Wall Street Journal* for August 9, 1998, reported: "As far back as the 1960s he had ties with reputed racketeers who had operated out of pre-Castro Cuba and who later forged an anti-Castro alliance with the CIA." Recarey openly boasted of a close connection with Santos Trafficante, the Florida mob boss who was a key organizer of the Mafia-CIA compact to assassinate Fidel Castro.

A certified public accountant, Recarey kick-started a health maintenance organization (HMO) by signing up 10,000 Cuban political prisoners as they stepped off planes in Miami after being released. This was the beginning of International Medical Centers (IMC). Trafficante helped with some short-term financing, and under the Reagan-Bush administration's beneficial gaze IMC became the largest HMO in the nation. As might be expected, there was a quid pro quo: IMC funneled funds to the Nicaraguan Contras under the cover of medical aid. In 1985, when Recarey needed a waiver of Medicare rules to expand his enterprise, which was largely dependent on federal programs for the elderly, he put in a call to Jeb Bush. The vice president's son hustled the Department of Health & Human Services, saying, according to later congressional testimony, that "America could trust Mike Recarey" to waive the regulation that no more than 50 percent of an HMO's revenues could come from Medicare payments. As chronicled in the *Miami Herald* on March 4, 1988, Recarey reciprocated by setting up Jeb Bush's real estate firm, Bush Realty, to turn a $250,000 profit on a deal Bush was negotiating for IMC. Although the deal fell through, Recarey paid Bush $75,000 for his trouble.

The money was well spent, for Recarey had been jailed briefly for failing to file income tax returns and had a dossier of fraud allegations resulting from prior dealings with Florida hospitals, and probably could not have gotten the waiver without Bush's intercession. With the waiver, IMC's income from Medicare checks vaulted to 80 percent of receipts. When it collapsed in a billion-dollar Medicare fraud in 1987, IMC was the largest recipient of Medicare payments in the United States. Thousands of geriatric Floridians never received the medical care for which IMC had been paid. Federal investigators theorized that a hefty chunk of the millions that disappeared under Recarey's creative accounting was diverted to the Contras.

To the end, Miguel Recarey's contacts of influence bestowed special privileges on him. Although under indictment for massive fraud and racketeering in the IMC debacle, he was allowed to keep his passport, obtain passports for his children, and sell off assets that included condos, Ferraris and BMWs, which ordinarily are frozen. And he received a $2.2 million tax refund that was expedited just in time for his fleeing the United States, presumably for Venezuela, in 1987.

It was in 1989 that Jeb Bush interceded with his father on behalf of Orlando Bosch, whom he probably perceived as a freedom fighter. But the bloody trail that Bosch laid down, with all its innocent victims, casts him indubitably in the role of terrorist. The story began two decades earlier, in 1968, when Bosch, totally frustrated that the CIA schemes to overthrow Castro had failed miserably, morphed from baby doctor to mad bomber. He created a terrorist cell called

Cuban Power that, like the religious lunatic on the train in *On the Twentieth Century*, left trademark red, white and blue stickers at the scene of the crime. On May 31, 1968, a Japanese freighter docked at Tampa and a British merchantman under way off Key West were wracked by explosions. The following day in Miami, a man calling himself Ernesto staged a press conference condemning countries doing business with Cuba—which were most nations—to warn that "other ships are going to explode." Although wearing a hood, Ernesto was easily identified as the local fanatic, Orlando Bosch. That summer Cuban Power terrorism spread to Los Angeles, where the British consulate, the Mexico Tourist Department and an Air France office were bombed, and to Manhattan, where the diplomatic agencies of six countries were hit. However, on September 16, 1968, Bosch was caught red-handed by FBI agents acting on an inside tip as he fired on the Polish motor ship *Polanica* at berth in Miami harbor. Convicted of terrorism, Bosch was locked up in a federal penitentiary.

Upon his release four years later, an unrepentant Bosch vowed to "internationalize the war." By early 1975 he was in Chile, where General Pinochet put him up in a government guest house while he planned with the DINA secret police to put into action Operation Condor, a pan-hemispheric terrorism campaign against the socialist enemy. In early 1976, according to the *Washington Post* on November 22 of that year, an informant tipped off Miami police lieutenant Michael Lynch that Bosch was plotting the bombing assassination of Henry Kissinger, along with his deputy William Rogers, during a forthcoming visit to Costa Rica. Kissinger had angered Bosch by quietly negotiating with the Cuban government to end the trade embargo. Lynch notified Costa Rican authorities, and four days before Kissinger's arrival in March, Bosch, who had entered the country on a false passport, was detained. "We offered to send him back," Foreign Minister Gonzalo Facio Segreda said of his contact with the U.S. State Department, "but the reply was that they were not interested."

Many lives would have been saved if the State Department had not so cavalierly waved off the Costa Rican offer. Three months later in a mountain lodge in Bonao in the Dominican Republic, Bosch founded an umbrella group of Cuban exile ultras, Coordination of United Revolutionary Organizations (CORU). If Bosch could not be directly linked to the Letelier assassination that September, he was definitely implicated in the bombing of the Cuban airliner a month later. On October 6, 1976, Cubana Airlines Flight 455 left Trinidad, stopped at Barbados, then took off for Cuba. The plane blew apart in flight, and all seventy-three on board perished.

On a journalistic visit to Havana in 1987, I stopped by the Museo de la Marcha del Pueblo Combatiente (Museum of the March of the Fighting People), a modern white structure with slatted windows housing exhibits memorializing epochal events in the revolutionary struggle. Prominent among them was a Flight 455 display: the pilot's cap and logbook of the Canadian-built aircraft recovered from the crash scene, a group portrait of the national fencing team that was on board, a photo of the mass funeral for the victims attended by a million people. Flight 455 is to the Cubans what 9/11 has become to Americans. This was emphasized when Fidel Castro immediately condemned the 9/11 attacks.

The Flight 455 case was solved when two men who had deplaned in Barbados, Freddy Lugo and Hernando Ricardo, were questioned by the authorities after joking about the bombing in a taxicab. The pair fingered Bosch and a veteran terrorist named Luis Posada as the masterminds of the mass murder, who supplied the two bombs they planted on the doomed aircraft. Bosch and Posada, who were based in Caracas at the time, were convicted by Venezuelan authorities. For eleven years Bosch languished in prison. Then, six weeks after the arrival in Caracas of a new U.S. ambassador, Bosch was retried and acquitted.

This might have been chalked up to coincidence were it not for the identity of the envoy, Otto Reich. A member of a landed-gentry family in Cuba that fled the revolution, Reich was a die-hard Castro hater and perfervid anticommunist. From 1983 to 1986, he had headed a Contra support program out of an ad hoc branch of the State Department vaguely called the Office of Public Diplomacy. According to *The New Yorker* on October 14, 2002, it was a propaganda mill pure and simple, leaking such fabrications as the Soviets were shipping MiG fighters to a Sandinista government that was into drug trafficking. A 1987 inquiry by the U.S. comptroller general, when the Iran-Contra scandal was breaking, concluded that Reich's shop had "engaged in prohibited, covert propaganda activities."

Although Reich has denied taking a special interest in the case, Bosch himself thought he had. Shortly after his cell door opened, Bosch expressed his thanks to his "compatriot." There is no doubt Reich took a special interest in the processing of Bosch's visa application once he was freed. Declassified notes appended to the application reveal that Reich reported that a Cuban assassination team had entered Caracas gunning for Bosch, whose friends would be able to extract him from the country at a moment's notice. Undoubtedly this bit of dramatics was designed to expedite the visa processing. But Bosch couldn't wait for the visa. In February 1988 he was nabbed at the Miami International Airport for illegal entry. The U.S. Justice Department charged him with parole violation stemming from the 1968 *Polanica* incident, ruled him incorrigible, and ordered him deported.

That was when Jeb Bush stepped in. At the time he was campaign manager for a Cuban-American candidate for Congress, Ileana Ros-Lehtinen (who remains in the House of Representatives). Both saw Bosch not as a serial terrorist but as a resolute fighter against Castro. On July 17, 1990, after young Bush took up Bosch's cause with his father, the president, the Justice Department deportation order was overturned. Upon his release, an unrepentant Dr. Death called a press conference to denounce the terms of his liberty, which included the renunciation of terrorism. He was quoted by the *New York Times* on July 18, 1990, as snarling, "They purchased the chain, but they don't have the monkey." He never did renounce terrorism, nor was he ever deported. He reinvented himself, becoming the Rembrandt of Little Havana whose paintings are snatched up by admirers.

It happened with the suddenness of a thunderclap. On March 18, 2003, as the countdown to George W. Bush's invasion of Iraq entered its final phase, Fidel Castro cracked down hard on internal dissent by rounding up seventy-five writers, journalists and democracy activists who had not hewed to the party line, and, after swift trials in which informers testified, punished them with stiff sentences. With this panicky move Castro slammed the door, at least temporarily, on an escalating movement in the U.S. Congress to lift the forty-four-year-old economic embargo, establish trade and tourism, and generally soften relations. But with Bush's vow to dispatch Saddam Hussein nearing reality, Castro saw himself as an addition to the "axis of evil" short list for regime change.

Ever since the 1961 Bay of Pigs invasion by an exile force commanded by the CIA, Cuba has been edgy about Washington's intentions. During a 1981 trip to Havana, I stood on the Santa Maria beach with an official of the Ministry of the Exterior, looking northward, when suddenly a speedboat appeared on the horizon and headed straight for us. "Here comes Alpha 66," I quipped, with reference to the most deadly of the exile action groups. The official laughed, but it was a nervous laugh. Under the Clinton administration, a trend toward constructive engagement with Cuba had developed. Relations between the two countries hit a speed bump in 1996. At a time when the administration had negotiated migration and narcotics control accords (Cuba became an invaluable ally in the war on drugs), Cuban MiGs shot down two small planes belonging to Brothers to the Rescue, an exile group whose overt purpose was to aid people fleeing Cuba by boat. It seemed like a wanton act of brutality, and was largely reported that way in the American media. But Castro had every reason to suspect that the Brothers had an agenda that was not exactly humanitarian. The Brothers' head was Jose Basulto, a survivor of the Bay of Pigs who, as reported by the *New York Times* in August 1962, participated in a boat shelling of the seaside Hotel Rosita de Horneda with the aim of killing Castro as he attended a reception inside. In the mid-1980s, according to the *Wall Street Journal* of August 6, 1988, Basulto was "coordinating" medical aid to the Nicaraguan Contras under the cover of "construction superintendent" of International Medical Centers, the HMO of Jeb Bush's corrupt business associate, Miguel Recarey. In the weeks leading up to the Brothers incident, Basulto sent planes over Havana dropping propaganda leaflets. The flights were so provocative that Castro fired off notes to Washington warning "deadly force" would be used if they were not stopped, in effect laying out a no-fly zone.

In the aftermath of the shootdown, it was determined that both planes came perilously close to Cuban airspace, and one even briefly entered it. Bill Clinton, pressured by hawks in his administration to respond militarily, consulted with his ranking national security advisors and the chairman of the Joint Chiefs of Staff, General John Shalikashvili, on whether to launch a cruise missile attack or air strikes. Shalikashvili said no, but Clinton, still simmering, sent a diktat to Castro threatening retaliation should any more planes be shot down. An angry Congress passed the Helms-Burton Bill, which aimed at strangling the Cuban economy by penalizing corporations doing business in the United States that did business with Cuba as well. Spain's Melia hotel chain, one of the world's largest, simply abandoned plans for expansion into the United States rather than give up its Cuban resorts, an example that others would follow. In time, emotions cooled and practicality took over. Members of Congress from farm states, many of them Republicans, pushed to sell grain and corn to Cuba. The manufacturing sector followed suit, lobbying for the opportunity to export appliances and other products. Even Cuban rights activists urged an easing of restrictions. "The more American citizens in the streets of Cuban cities," reasoned Elizardo Sanchez, a commanding figure in the movement, "the better for the cause of a more open society."

The trend toward constructive engagement picked up momentum with the May 2002 visit of former president Jimmy Carter in his customary role as an ambassador for reconciliation. Carter freely roamed the island, talking with the locals, and was allowed to meet privately with members of the Varela Project, a dissident group that had collected more than 11,000 signatures on a petition for a referendum on political and human rights. But hovering over the occasion was the shadow of a belligerent George W. Bush, then in the process of trying to prove that Iraq possessed weapons of mass destruction. A week before Carter's trip, Undersecretary of State John Bolton, in the course of a dinner address, accused Cuba of sending technical data to rogue states and developing a germ warfare capability. The charges, for which Bolton offered no substantiation, were obviously designed to undermine Carter's visit as well as plant the notion that Cuba possessed WMD just like Saddam Hussein. While being briefed by U.S. intelligence before departure, Carter asked whether there was any evidence that Bolton's allegations were true. "The answer from our experts on terrorism was no," Carter said upon arrival in Havana. The ex-president made a point of touring the Center for Genetic Engineering and Biotechnology, which engaged in medical research. He confronted its director, Luis Herrera, who flatly denied any bioterrorism research and offered a full inspection of the laboratory. As reported in *Pravda* on May 14, 2002, Bolton finally had to admit that he had relied on rumors passed on by anti-Castro exiles in Miami. It was this kind of recklessness that was to characterize President Bush's struggle to "prove" Hussein had WMD, but Castro must have thought he was being set up. Interestingly, among the experts rebutting Bolton on Cuba was Christian Westermann, the same Westermann who would again incur Bolton's wrath by testifying that he resisted pressure to alter his report that Iraq had no WMD.

If Castro had harbored any doubt about the malevolent intent of George W. Bush toward him, it was dispelled in early 2001 when the president, acting on the recommendation of Jeb Bush, appointed Otto Reich, Orlando Bosch's benefactor, to the post of Assistant Secretary of State for Western Hemisphere Affairs. It was a jaw-breaking title for the most influential office on Latin America within the State Department. Democrats on the Senate Foreign Relations Committee recognized Reich as ideologically over the top and refused to hold hearings on his nomination, twice returning his name to the White House. Progressive think tanks ran off batches of press releases, portraying him as a dangerous fanatic with a dark past. An alarmed Cuban government tagged him as a "terrorist" and "mafioso." After a year of stalemate, Bush pulled off a recess appointment that was not subject to confirmation. At his swearing-in ceremony, which was attended by Colin Powell and Senator Jesse Helms, Reich was his usual in-your-face self. According to *The New Yorker* for October 14, 2002, he couldn't resist taking a shot at his critics: "They said that I can't make rational decisions because of my ideology. Well, they are not saying that anymore, because I had them all arrested this morning." The transcript didn't record whether anyone laughed.

Reich quickly confirmed himself as a loose cannon. In September 2002 when a Midwestern delegation traveled to Havana for an agribusiness trade fair, he insulted everyone, including Minnesota Governor Jesse Ventura, by sarcastically warning them not to indulge in "sexual tourism" while there. In April 2002, he tried to pull off a regime change in Venezuela, his old stomping ground. An amalgam of business, military and wealthy elites was attempting to depose President Hugo Chavez, a democratically elected champion of the people who was friendly with Fidel Castro and sold him discounted oil. At first all went well: A business executive named Pedro Carmona was installed as the new president. To emphasize that a coup had succeeded, Reich summoned a number of Latin American envoys to his office, told them that Chavez had resigned, and asked them to join the United States in recognizing the new government. According to *The New Yorker* article, the only problem was that Chavez hadn't resigned, and Carmona was heading toward dissolving the National Assembly, the country's parliament.

Reich phoned Carmona, telling him dissolution would be a "stupid thing to do." However, support for the vacillating Carmona was melting away, and within two days Chavez was back in power. With egg on its face, the Bush administration scrambled to endorse a resolution by the Organization of American States condemning the coup as a breach of Venezuela's constitution. But Reich couldn't restrain himself from meddling further. During the violent anti-Chavez demonstrations that followed the coup's collapse, the master of black propaganda spread the lie that "foreign paramilitary forces" believed to be Cuban were helping disperse the demonstrators.

At the same time that George W. Bush was staging his extravaganza on the aircraft carrier on May Day 2003 to boast that the Iraq war was effectively over, Fidel Castro in Havana was also engaging in hyperbole. Branding the dissidents rounded up before the war as "mercenaries on the payroll of Bush's Hitler-like government," he contended that Bush was poised to invade Cuba. The mercenaries reference was to the head of the U.S. Interests Section in Havana, James Cason, who earlier had roamed the island encouraging the dissidents, awarding grants-in-aid to some. It was revealing that the one dissident Castro didn't touch was the most famous of them all, the charismatic Oswaldo Paya, head of the Varela Project. During his visit, Jimmy Carter hailed Paya in a speech broadcast to every Cuban household, and Paya was awarded the European Union's Sakharov Prize for human rights. In a crucial way, *Time* reported on May 19, 2003, Paya was different. He kept clear of James Cason, and studiously avoided giving any perception of collaborating with the United States. Apparently Castro was more spooked by George Bush than Oswaldo Paya. Undoubtedly, there will come a time when Castro will release the dissidents—following the 1998 visit of Pope John Paul II, he freed 299 political prisoners.

But any amnesty probably must await the removal of the Bush menace as personified by archenemy Otto Reich, the master of blatant intrigue. Just like his neocon colleagues in the Bush administration who inspired the invasion of Iraq with a vision of American dominance in the region, Reich savors the promise of an Americanized Cuba. The passwords "liberty" and "democracy" fall freely from his lips. Dominating his office in the State Department is an almost life-size statue of Simon Bolivar, the nineteenth century liberator of Latin American countries who is revered in the region. The intended symbolism is inescapable. But Reich seems blissfully unaware of Bolivar's most telling saying: "The USA seems destined by Providence to plague us with all kinds of evils in the name of liberty."

In *The New Yorker* issue of November 17, 2003, General Wesley Clark recounted that when he visited the Pentagon shortly after 9/11 an old colleague, a three-star general, confided to him that Defense Secretary Donald Rumsfeld and his team planned to use the attacks as a pretext for going to war against Iraq. "They made the decision to attack Iraq sometime soon after 9/11," Clark said. "So rather than searching for a solution to a problem, they had the solution, and their difficulty was to make it appear as though it was in response to a problem." A couple of months later, the same general told Clark that the Bush team, unable or unwilling to fight the terrorists responsible for the attacks, had devised a five-year plan to topple the regimes in Iraq, Syria, Lebanon, Libya, Somalia, Iran and Sudan.

Castro is sure Cuba is somewhere on the list. How ironic that the one nation that has never harbored terrorists, and indeed has been the victim of American-based terrorists, should wind up a target.

5

DRY DRUNK

After the 1972 election, in which Richard Nixon deflected the Watergate issue to gain reelection, he appointed George H. W. Bush chairman of the Republican National Committee, which required a move to Washington. At the time, George W., age twenty-six, was on one of his absences from the Texas Air National Guard, which he had joined to escape the Vietnam War. The family had gathered for the holiday at Poppy's newly rented house. George W. decided to visit a friend, and the two imbibed heavily. What ensued when he drove home was reported in *Time* magazine on July 31, 1989. Drunk and driving erratically, George W. barreled the car into a neighbor's garbage can, which clung to the car wheel. He drove down the street with the metal garbage can clanging noisily and slapping on the pavement right up until he made the turn into the driveway of his parents' home. Once inside, he was given word that Poppy, who had been reading in the den, wanted to see him. Angry and flushed from the liquor, George W. barged in. "I hear you're looking for me," he said belligerently. "You wanna go mano a mano right here?" Jeb Bush interceded, and the moment passed.

The implications of that shameful moment have not passed. It is, of course, shocking that the man who is now president of the United States would have, in a booze-induced rage, challenged his own father to a fistfight with the full intent of doing him violence. But the question that is critically relevant today is whether George W. Bush is a "dry drunk." Katherine Van Wormer, professor of social work at the University of Northern Iowa and co-author of *Addiction Treatment: A Strengths Perspective*, elucidates: "*Dry drunk* is a slang term used by members and supporters of Alcoholics Anonymous and substance abuse counselors to describe the recovering alcoholic who is no longer drinking, one who is dry, but whose thinking is clouded. Such an individual is said to be dry but not truly sober. Such an individual tends to go to extremes." Pronounced personality traits featured during the drinking period hang over into the nondrinking present, and often are more accented than vestigial.

Bush gave up drinking in 1986 as he turned forty. He described himself as a "heavy drinker," but was in denial that he was actually an alcoholic, as so many alcoholics do. The playing out of his epiphany is recounted by Texas newspaper reporter Bill Minutaglio in his biography *First Son: George W. Bush and the Bush Family Dynasty*, who identified the setting as Colorado's grand Broadmoor Hotel, where George and Laura Bush and two other couples had gathered for a party:

> That night the group assembled and the drinks flowed. Laura watched her husband. . . . Laura had seen this before, almost since they were married, the way that after a few drinks he'd think he was funnier than he really was. A thought would occur

to her, "Isn't that what every drunk thinks?" She had always felt that her husband was good at impulse and not introspection; he wasn't going to spend time trying to find out if he had a clinical problem with alcohol. She had said it was "necessary" to stop. It was almost a bad joke: *Choose me or Jim Beam.* Some people in West Texas clucked and said that she was tired of waiting at home when he was out, and when they heard that his all-time favorite musician was George Jones, "Old Possum," it was almost too perfect—Jones was the archetype of the boozy country singer single-mindedly insisting on fraying his syllables and his liver.

That evening the group split up, and Bush wound his way back to his room. The next morning it was as bad as ever. Bush woke up with a pounding, churning hangover but somehow managed to go for a run. If there were plans to go to the places the Midlanders normally liked to visit, maybe the Air Force Academy Chapel, they didn't seem appealing anymore after a night of drinking. He told Laura that he wasn't ever going to drink again.

And he didn't.

However, according to Van Wormer, the damage may already have been done because of Bush's long history of heavy drinking. It is fair to say that the incidents that have come to light are only the tip of the iceberg—or ice cubes, to be more precise—since learning about them sometimes can be a tricky business. As an example, when Bush was running for governor of Texas in 1998, rumors swirled that a drunk driving arrest lurked in his past. The question was doubly important because he had flatly denied any encounter with a police blotter other than when he was an undergraduate at Yale. On that occasion, he was roistering down the streets of New Haven just before Christmas when he snatched a wreath off a Macy's storefront. He was spotted by police officers, who questioned him, arrested him, and charged him with disorderly conduct. According to the *Dallas Morning News* of September 6, 1968, Bush trivialized the incident as a "college prank" after he "might have had a few

beers." It was not until a few days before the 2000 presidential election that Bush's luck finally ran out on the DUI story. A reporter,
Erin Fehlau, covering a trial in a Maine courthouse, was told by a
police officer that she had overheard a defense attorney and the
judge casually talking about the GOP candidate's arrest record.
Fehlau braced the attorney, who gave her a copy of the docket. Fehlau
checked the docket number with the courthouse, and also interviewed the officer who had made the arrest. The Arrest Record Card
showed that George W. Bush, who gave an address of P.O. Box 185,
Midland, Texas, was booked on September 4, 1976, by an Officer
Bridges for Operating Under the Influence. Bridges had observed
him driving unusually slowly and swerving, and Bush flunked a field
sobriety test. He pleaded guilty to a misdemeanor charge of drunk
driving and was fined $250, and his driving privileges were sus-
pended.

With the election only four days off and polls showing him with
only a slight lead over Al Gore, Bush faced the television cameras
with the look of a deer caught in the headlights. Bush admitted that
he had had "a few beers" at a bar in Kennebunkport, Maine, near
the family vacation home, and was arrested for drunk driving. "I
regret that it happened, but it did," he said. Bush knew that the
issue wasn't so much the arrest but the fact that he had previously
denied it, which tended to impeach his credibility. But then he intimated that Gore's camp had set up Erin Fehlau (which she stoutly
denied). "It was 24 years ago, and that's the interesting thing about
this: here we are with four days to go in the campaign and we're
discussing what happened 24 years ago," he complained in a surge
of paranoia. "I've got my suspicions. . . . I've got my suspicions."
The main reason Bush cited for not disclosing the arrest sooner was
he did not want to set a bad example for his twin daughters, Jenna

and Barbara. "I made the decision that, as a dad, I didn't want my girls doing the kinds of things I did," he said. But they did. Within a couple of months of dad assuming office, Jenna and Barbara had brushes with the law, trying to buy drinks in bars by flashing phony IDs. But the lying about a drunk driving arrest almost cost Bush the White House. He lost the popular vote to Gore by nearly half a million votes, only to be rescued by a Supreme Court coup.

When imbibing, Bush delighted in throwing digs at others that often amounted to hurtful humor. The *New York Times* of September 13, 1998, described this behavior circa 1970 when he was a weekend warrior with the Texas Air National Guard leading the bachelor's life in a Houston apartment:

> Sometimes his competitive, combative tendencies would surface—he would rock on his heels, bobbing, looking for a place to throw a dig, even at his father. His closest friends would say that when he drank too much he would try to be funny; he would think he was wickedly funny, but everything he said was distinctly unfunny. His friends knew the story about the time at the society party, with the guests turned out in elegant attire, when he might have tossed back one too many. He wobbled his way through the fete, spied an older woman who was a close friend of his parents, and blurted, "So—what's sex life like after fifty, anyway?"

A nasty incident during his 1978 run for U.S. Congress in West Texas demonstrated how thin-skinned Bush could get. His Democratic opponent was State Senator Kent Hance, an aggressive good old boy native to the area. On the hustings Hance depicted Bush as a carpetbagging fancy-pants representing the Northeast elite establishment. Bush countered by depicting himself as a hard-line conservative. He said he was opposed to sanctions against apartheid South Africa and contended that the appointment of Andrew Young, a black man, as ambassador to the United Nations had been "a mistake." He also condemned the Equal Rights Amendment and national health insurance. Only weeks before the election Bush and Hance engaged in a debate in an Odessa restaurant. Bush was smarting over being attacked by Hance on the alcohol issue. Bush's booze habit was an open secret in the area, but he had gone over the top by placing an ad in the Texas Tech newspaper inviting students, most of whom were too young to legally drink, to a Bush Bash party featuring free beer. Hance hopped on the blunder, saying, "Mr. Bush used some of his vast sums of money in an attempt, evidently, to persuade young college students to vote for and support him by offering free alcohol to them."

At this point, the moderator of the debate, a local radio talk show host named Mel Turner, changed the subject. As told by Bill Minutaglio:

> Turner, speaking for a good chunk of West Texas, wanted to know if the young Bush was a tool of some shadow government; it was the same thing people had confronted his father with when they had called him a "tool of the eastern kingmakers": "Are you involved in, or do you know anybody involved in, one-world government or the Trilateral Commission?" Bush was fuming. "I won't be persuaded by anyone, including my father," he said, with a biting tone in his voice. On the way out of the restaurant, Bush was still livid. He refused to shake hands with Turner. "You asshole," Turner heard him hiss as he walked by. Turner had been leaning toward voting for Bush but had changed his mind: "Hance was much better at talking to the average workingman. Bush never worked a day in his life. Bush was born with a silver boot up his ass. Everything was handed to him."

Bush lost the election; it wasn't even close.

In *First Son*, Minutaglio also recounted how Bush reacted to perceived slights while under the influence. In April 1986 the vice president's son was in Dallas attending to the demise of his oil firm, Spectrum 7. He went to a Mexican restaurant and spied Al Hunt, the Washington bureau chief of the *Wall Street Journal*, there with his family, including his four-year-old son. In the nation's capital, the latest issue of *The Washingtonian* magazine was circulating. It contained predictions on who would be on the 1988 presidential ballot by top political pundits such as Sam Donaldson, John McLaughlin, Rowland Evans, Judy Woodruff and Al Hunt. The only mention of Hunt read, "Al Hunt, *Wall Street Journal*: Kemp and Indiana Senator Richard Lugar against Hart and Robb." Nothing about George H. W. Bush, the vice president. As Minutaglio described the scene:

> Now Hunt spotted the thirty-nine-year-old George W. Bush winding over to his table. "You no good fucking sonofabitch, I will never fucking forget what you wrote," he heard Bush sputtering as he stepped up to Hunt and his family. Hunt stared at him, nonplussed. He didn't know Bush very well, had hardly seen him around the campaigns or at the White House. Lingering for thirty seconds by Hunt's table, Bush mentioned *The Washingtonian*. Hunt was confused. He hadn't thrown any darts, let alone any hatchets, at Bush's father. He also assumed that Bush had been drinking heavily, that "he was quite clearly lubricated." And after Bush left Hunt and his family alone, a thought blinked in Hunt's head: "This is a guy who's got problems."

Contrary to Hunt's prediction, in 1988 Poppy Bush was nominated as the presidential standard-bearer for the GOP. By that time, George W. had sworn off the bottle, but his mean conduct continued, symptomatic of the dry drunk. He moved to Washington, the better to deal with media on his father's behalf. As Minutaglio put it, "The Washington reporters had come to a conclusion in the months that George W. had been in the incestuous Beltway loop of aides, staffers, and spin doctors: He had started in Washington with a cockiness that boiled over into hot-tempered arrogance and a special contempt reserved for members of the media who presumed to probe his father's character." The reference was to philandering. Rumors persisted that Poppy had a long-standing affair with his secretary, Jennifer Fitzgerald, that at one point was consummated in a borrowed Swiss chalet. The rumors were strong enough that *Newsweek* and *U.S. News & World Report* printed them. While Poppy issued a pious denial, George W. turned downright nasty. A veteran White House correspondent recalled that young Bush would mutter "No comment, asshole" and "look at you like you had just crawled up out of a hole in the ground" just for asking a question he didn't like. In fact, "asshole" seems to be Bush's rote gutter appellation. During Campaign 2000, an open mike on a speech platform caught him pointing out to Dick Cheney a *New York Times* reporter whose articles hadn't pleased him: "That's the asshole."

On the matter of drug abuse, which certainly would contribute to the dry drunk syndrome, George W. has not exactly been forthcoming. When running for governor in Texas in 1994, a *Houston Chronicle* reporter openly posed whether he had experimented with illegal drugs. "Maybe I did, maybe I didn't. What's the relevance?" Bush is quoted in the *Chronicle* on May 3, 1994. The following day he skirmished with another reporter on the drug question. "I just don't think it matters. Did I behave irresponsibly as a kid at times? Sure did. You bet," was his answer as published by the *Texarkana Gazette*. Ironically, the name of his campaign plane, a King Air turboprop, that had transported him between the two cities was *Accountability One*. At the outset of Campaign 2000 he bristled when asked the same question, refusing to allow even a limited hangout.

Perhaps he was afraid that a certain videotape would surface that would incriminate him in a cocaine buy. In his 1994 book *Compromised: Clinton, Bush and the CIA*, former CIA contract agent Terry Reed described how Barry Seal, a veteran drug-running pilot and FBI informant (he was later assassinated by the Colombian Medellin drug cartel), had told him he had "insurance" in the form of proof that the "Bush boys" were doing heavy drugs. As Campaign 2000 loomed and George W. was the Republican front-runner, Reed elaborated on the subject to Michael Ruppert, an ex–Los Angeles cop who publishes a newsletter called *From the Wilderness*. As Ruppert tells it in the July 28, 1999, issue, in 1985 through Seal

> the FBI had inserted a female undercover agent into the inner circle of Medellin Cartel founder Pablo Escobar. Her name was Darlene Novinger, and she got very close to an Escobar cousin named Steve Plata. Well, thanks to the "uc," as undercovers are called, Barry Seal and Terry Reed were sent on a drug sting to meet some wealthy Texans who were flying into Tamiami Airport outside of Miami, Florida to pick up a couple of kilos of [cocaine] powder for a party. Well, it turns out that the wealthy Texans were George W. and Jeb Bush, who flew in on the family King Air to pick up the cocaine themselves. Hidden DEA [Drug Enforcement Administration] cameras filmed the whole incident, including the tail number of the aircraft and both Bushes' participation. According to Reed, no one knew in advance who the buyers were. Reed states that he has both the tail number of the aircraft and the DEA case file number and that he strongly expects that tape to turn up during the 2000 presidential campaign.

As it turned out, the only substance abuse record that turned up was George W.'s drunk driving conviction.

But the Bush brothers have reason to worry that the truth about their alleged drug dealing will someday surface, crippling George W. as president. Reed disclosed the tail number of the King Air 200, a turboprop executive aircraft, as N6308F, in aviation circles Zero-Eight-Foxtrot. Federal Aviation Administration (FAA) registration records, obtained by Ruppert, reflected that in 1985 the craft was on lease to the state of Texas. But the DEA case file is buried, and with it the prime exhibit: the videotape. So the mystery of Zero-Eight-Foxtrot remains just that. But it is possible to put the mystery in some context. In 1985 Vice President George Bush was the White House point man for aid to the Nicaraguan Contras fighting against their elected government. The veep was close to the CIA, which was covertly providing logistical and strategic support to the Contras. As later came out in congressional hearings, the CIA supply planes took guns south and brought drugs north. Jeb Bush was wheeling and dealing with Miguel Recarey, the corrupt Miami entrepreneur who was a conduit for money to the Contras. And 1985 was the year before George W. would claim deliverance from the bottle.

The idea that George W. is a dry drunk originated with Alan Bisbort, a columnist for the *Hartford Advocate*, who lost his own brother to alcoholism. "For the record," Bisbort wrote in his column of September 24, 2002, "Bush claims to have stopped drinking for reasons that change each time he is asked about his substance-abusing past. Let's say he started experimenting with alcohol, as per the natural norm, at 16 at prep school, and he began getting regularly wasted at Yale. That would mean that Bush drank steadily 'heavily' for at least 22 years." As Bisbort pointed out in the case of his brother, sustained heavy drinking causes irreversible and dramatic changes in metabolism and brain chemistry. At the same time, "my brother was a functioning member of society. He held jobs, paid his rent and bills, and he made heroic efforts to beat his cursed addiction. He took the 12 steps more times than Stallone climbed those steps in 'Rocky.'"

With Bush, Bisbort went on, "the question is then begged: How did he, at age 58, get so fumble-tongued, incapable of stringing more than two coherent sentences together, snippily irritable with anyone who dares disagree with him or even ask a question, poutily turning his back on the democratically elected president of one of our most important allies because of something one of his underlings said about him (Germany's Schroeder, of course), listlessly in need of constant vacations and rest, dangerously obsessed with one thing (Iraq) to the exclusion of all other things?"

Noting that Congress was in default in straightening up Bush, Bisbort exhorted citizens to take over. "George W. Bush needs an intervention. Let's be his interveners. Let's raise our sober voices. Let's ask questions, demand more than temper tantrums and pouting from the Commander in Chief. Let's do this before it's too late and a dry drunk's dream of glory becomes our national nightmare."

Bisbort's scary thesis caught the eye of Professor Van Wormer of Northern Iowa University, who put her considerable experience in the field of addiction treatment into an analysis of Bush as a dry drunk. She had been predisposed to believe there was something to it by Bush's choice of words. "It was when I started noticing the extreme language that colored President Bush's speeches," Van Wormer wrote in the newsletter *Counterpunch* on October 11, 2002, "that I began to wonder. First there were the terms 'crusade' and 'infinite justice' that were later withdrawn. Next came 'evildoers,' 'axis of evil,' and 'regime change,' terms that have almost become clichés in the mass media. Something about the polarized thinking and the obsessive repetition reminded me of many of the recovering alcoholics/addicts I had treated." Van Wormer continued, "I flinched at the single-mindedness and ego- and ethnocentricity in the President's speeches. Since words are the tools, the representations of thought, I wondered what Bush's choice of words said about where he was coming from. Or where we would be going."

Next Van Wormer asked: What is the dry drunk syndrome? She listed its traits:

Exaggerated self-importance and pomposity
Grandiose behavior
A rigid, judgmental outlook
Impatience
Childish behavior
Irresponsible behavior
Irrational rationalization
Projection
Overreaction

In Van Wormer's analysis, Bush has all these traits except exaggerated self-importance, which is because as leader of the most powerful nation on earth it is impossible to exaggerate. "His power, in fact, is such that if he collapses into paranoia, a large part of the world will collapse with him," Van Wormer wrote. "Unfortunately, there are some indications of paranoia in statements such as the following: 'We must be prepared to stop rogue states and their terrorist clients before they are able to threaten or use weapons of mass destruction against the United States and our allies and friends.'" Van Wormer said that the trait of *projection* is evidenced here as well, projection of the fact that we are ready to attack another nation that may not be so inclined.

According to Van Wormer, Bush's tendency to polarize is symptomatic of the classic addictive thinking pattern — "either you are with us or against us." All-or-nothing thinking is commonly found in recovering alcoholics and addicts. Such a worldview traps people in a pattern of destructive behavior. Obsessive thought patterns are also pronounced in persons prone to addiction. "There are organic reasons due to brain chemistry irregularities: messages in one part of the brain become stuck there," Van Wormer says. "This leads to maddening repetition of thoughts. President Bush seems unduly focused on getting revenge on Saddam Hussein ('He tried to kill my Dad'), leading the country into war."

Grandiosity enters the picture as well. "What Bush proposed to Congress," Van Wormer explained, "is not the right to attack one country but a total shift in military policy: America would now have the right to take military action before the adversary even has the capacity to attack. This is in violation, of course, of international law as well as national precedent. How to explain this grandiose request? Jane Bryant Quinn provides the most commonly offered explanation in a recent *Newsweek* editorial, 'Iraq: It's the Oil, Stupid.' Many other opponents of the Bush doctrine similarly seek a rational motive behind the obsession over first, the war on terror and now, Iraq. I believe the explanation goes deeper than oil, that Bush's logic is being given too much credit; I believe his obsession is far more visceral." This couples with journalist Bob Woodward's disclosure that Bush, by his own admission, makes decisions based on gut feelings. In other words, he doesn't think things through, perhaps because he is incapable of doing so. That is ominous news for Americans who after 9/11 defaulted on thinking for themselves and allowed Bush to do it for them.

Van Wormer's portrayal of Bush as a dry drunk raises the question of what cerebral pathology might have been behind the meticulously choreographed theatrics of the tail-hook landing on the aircraft carrier's deck to announce, prematurely as it turned out, that major combat had ceased, and the "surprise" touch-and-go landing at Baghdad airport on Thanksgiving Day for a photo op with the troops. One benefit is that the Republicans will have film footage in the can for Campaign 2004 depicting Bush as a bold commander concerned for his troops. Although it was billed as a singular event, the fact is that a host of former presidents have taken such sudden, stealth trips. In January 1943, during the height of World War II, a wheelchair-bound Franklin Delano Roosevelt ventured to Morocco to meet with U.S. commanders prosecuting the campaign against the German Afrika Corps. In 1952 President-elect Dwight D. Eisenhower left New York under cover of darkness on a 47-hour flight to Korea in an attempt to expedite the end of the Korean War, which he was about to inherit. During the Vietnam War, Lyndon B. Johnson made a secret trip to the U.S. military complex at Cam Ranh Bay to bolster the troops. In March 2000, Bill Clinton flew into Pakistan despite concerns that al-Qaida had him marked; he performed a sleight of hand of sorts by switching planes during his departure from India for Islamabad.

The idea that Bush would politicize a photo op with the troops already had been sounded in the first television spot taken out by the Republican National Committee. Flashing the words "terrorist" and "self-defense" in crimson, the ad had Bush asking what was intended to be a rhetorical question: "Since when have terrorists and tyrants announced their intentions, politely putting us on notice before they strike?" But lumping al-Qaida in with Saddam Hussein was a deception — they had nothing to do with each other. In point of fact, the Iraq war diversion allowed al-Qaida to metastasize, its ranks swelling around the world, new leaders being bred. Richard Clarke, the former U.S. counterterrorism chief, told Ted Koppel that although some al-Qaida leaders are being eliminated, "we're breeding new ones — ones we don't know about and will be harder to find." On the very day that Bush was showboating at the Baghdad airport, pictured wearing a military jacket marked ARMY, surrounded by beaming soldiers and holding an ersatz Thanksgiving turkey—"His eyes were glistening," a gullible CBS reporter noted—British police were doing something concrete in the war on terrorism, arresting without fanfare two al-Qaida suspects with explosives in their possession.

As a World War II veteran and ten-year FBI agent who has come under fire in the service of this nation, I suspect that Bush has a deep psychological need to posture as a macho commander in chief. In 1968, when about to graduate from Yale, which meant his education exemption from the military draft would end, he was determined not to put himself in harm's way in Vietnam. His first inclination was to relocate to Canada, then a haven for draft dodgers, but he feared it might adversely affect his father's U.S. Senate aspirations. So, through political influence, he found shelter from the war in the Texas Air National Guard despite the fact that there were no slots open and he scored low on the entrance exam. As journalist Molly Ivins has drolly observed, the Texas Air National Guard at the time was chartered not to leave the state, so Bush spent the war "protecting El Paso from the Viet Cong." And drinking it up, she might have added. Bush was all for the war; he just wanted someone else to fight it. It is beyond reason why the American Legion and Veterans of Foreign Wars, organizations Bush is not eligible to join, would allow themselves to be used by him as platforms for his tough-guy speeches, applauding thunderously when he finishes, ignoring the fact that he has cut back on veterans' benefits.

Yet there are those in the rank and file of the Legion and the VFW who resent Bush as a "chickenhawk." In a letter to the editor of the *San Francisco Chronicle* on Veterans Day 2003, Vietnam War veteran Phil Scordelis turned apoplectic:

> I just witnessed the craven coward who occupies space in the White House visiting at Arlington National Cemetery, honoring U.S. veterans, and it turned my stomach. How dare that weak-willed, stupid man assume any vet with an inkling of sense would want him talking about our sacrifice. He ran like a dog when he had his chance to show his mettle, and now he is wasting American lives on a purposeless war. His actions have created far greater danger for the American people than we faced before he came to power. Can this nation last with such leaders? I fear not.

I was only slightly more temperate in a letter to *Vanity Fair* for August 2003: "If I were in the military today, I would resent having this slacker as my commander in chief."

Bush seems to be trying to exorcise the ghosts of his slacker past by obsessively identifying himself with the military of today, to reinvent himself as a warrior. He never saw a photo op with a military theme that he didn't like. He bounces from one base to another to be photographed rallying the troops (one exception: the Dover, Delaware, air base where the body bags from Iraq are brought home). On Veterans Day 2002 he had the effrontery to solemnly pose at the Vietnam War Memorial Wall, which honors the dead in a war he refused to fight. There is also the theory that some of Bush's strutting before the cameras, his belligerence, his insistence that he never is wrong derives from lowered self-esteem caused by living in his father's shadow. Katherine Van Wormer believes that he has an inferiority complex that colors his foreign policy. "The Bush biography reveals the story of a boy named for his father," Van Wormer wrote, "sent to the exclusive private school in the East where his father's reputation as star athlete and later war hero were still remembered. The younger George's achievements were dwarfed in the school's memory of his father. Athletically he could not achieve his father's laurels, being smaller and perhaps less strong. His drinking bouts and lack of intellectual gifts held him back." The stark contrast between his father's war record and his own deliberate lack of one was another contributing factor. Concludes Van Wormer: "It would be only natural that Bush would want to prove himself today, that he would feel somewhat uncomfortable following in his father's footsteps. I mention these things because when you follow his speeches, Bush seems bent on a personal crusade. One motive is to avenge his father. Another seems to be to prove himself to his father."

Van Wormer sums up: "George W. Bush manifests all the classic patterns of what alcoholics in recovery call 'the dry drunk.' His behavior is consistent with barely noticeable but meaningful brain damage brought on by years of heavy drinking and possible cocaine use. All the classic patterns of addictive thinking are here."

It is sobering indeed to know that this man is now power drunk.

6

CONDITION RED:
A VULNERABLE NATION

In February 2002 Tom Ridge, who is in charge of the Department of Homeland Security (DHS), took a helicopter tour over the site of the Winter Olympic games in Salt Lake City, which were to begin shortly. The games were considered a potential terrorism target of al-Qaida, which was known to have global reach. Upon alighting from the helicopter, Ridge gave his considered opinion to reporters: The Olympics venue was "the safest place in the world." A few days later Attorney General John Ashcroft flew over the site, spotting some ten holes in the security.

Ridge's unjustified complacency raised two questions absolutely critical to the public safety. Is a massive bureaucracy like the DHS productive or counterproductive? Does Tom Ridge have the credentials and smarts to make America as safe as possible from terrorist acts?

In the immediate aftermath of the 9/11 attacks there was an almost panicky climate in the country—do something, anything, to prevent future attacks. But there was no precedent; the mainland had never been attacked before. President Bush knew he had to make some move, any move, even if it was feel-good. So he seized upon the raw idea of Senator Joe Lieberman to form a superagency that would coordinate and supervise the twenty-two disparate domestic agencies that suddenly had one degree or another of responsibility for defending the home front. Only a few in Congress dared to voice the opinion that what was really needed was a leaner, meaner and more nimble operation. And so the DHS was created. It was the most sweeping reorganization of the government since 1947, when President Harry S. Truman merged the various branches of the armed forces into the Department of Defense (which had been the War Department) to better coordinate—at least in theory—the nation's defense against military threats. As the DHS describes its mission: "The new department's first priority is to protect the nation against further terrorist attacks. Component agencies will analyze threats and intelligence, guard our borders and airports, protect our critical infrastructure, and coordinate the response of our nation for future emergencies." Component agencies will analyze threats and intelligence? The DHS actually has formed a unit to undertake an intelligence function that overlaps with the established agencies: the CIA, the FBI, the National Security Agency and the military Defense Intelligence Agency. There is a certain redundancy in creating yet another intelligence outfit, a confusion of jurisdiction, one more agency in the loop. What is needed is streamlining, a central repository of data. The DHS is not charged with ferreting out terrorist cells—that is the task of the FBI.

As structured, the DHS is administratively top-heavy, being divided into five directorates. The largest is Border and Transportation Security, which is the umbrella for the Transportation Security Administration, the former U.S. Customs Service, the Bureau of

Citizenship and Immigration Services, Animal and Plant Health Inspection Service, and the Federal Law Enforcement Training Center. The prime responsibilities of this directorate are screening air passengers for contraband and protecting the nation's borders against the entry of potential terrorists. The second largest directorate is Emergency Preparedness and Response, whose assignment is the ability to prepare for, and recover from, terrorist attacks and natural disasters. The Science and Technology directorate coordinates research and development in preparing to respond to terrorists' weapons of mass destruction. The Information Analysis and Infrastructure Protection directorate merges the capacity to identify and assess a broad range of intelligence information on threats to the homeland under one roof, issuing warnings (Ridge's famous color codes) and taking appropriate preventive action. The fifth directorate is Management, which handles budget, management and personnel issues.

Hold on, there's more—several critical agencies are tucked into DHS. One is the Coast Guard, whose commandant reports directly to the DHS secretary (the post is now Cabinet level), Tom Ridge. But the Coast Guard also works closely with the Undersecretary of Border and Transportation Security, maintaining its status as a military service. Another is the Secret Service, which used to be under the Treasury Department; its primary mission is protection of the president and other government leaders, as well as securing designated national events like the Olympics. In addition, the Secret Service is responsible for investigating counterfeiting of U.S. currencies and credit card fraud. Then there is the Bureau of Citizenship and Immigration Services. No, it doesn't enforce immigration laws—that is charged to Border and Transportation Security. The Bureau, in its own words, "dedicates its full energies to providing efficient immigration services and easing the transition to American citizenship," which on the face of it has nothing to do with terrorism. Then there is the Office of State and Local Government Coordination, which handles liaison between local, state and federal governments and their first responders and emergency services, which deals with attacks after they happen. And the Office of Private Sector Liaison, which provides a direct line of communication with the business community with its security concerns.

Who is the man trying to get his arms around this 800-pound gorilla? Secretary Tom Ridge is not a security professional; he is a politician. He was on George W. Bush's short list for vice president, and the DHS post is his consolation prize. Ridge is a Vietnam veteran, a Harvard-trained lawyer and a former congressman with a wooden personality. While in Congress he was viewed as a moderate pro-choice Republican with an independent streak. But all that changed in 1993 when, in running for governor of Pennsylvania, he became a law-and-order demagogue. He capitalized on the tragic case of Reginald McFadden, a commuted felon who went on a homicide spree in New York after being released from prison, by tarring his Democratic opponent with the type of Willie Horton ads that the senior George Bush used against Michael Dukakis in the 1988 presidential contest. Upon taking office, Ridge called a special session of the legislature to push through a basket of draconian anticrime laws, a number of which proved ineffectual or were ruled unconstitutional. He insisted that juveniles be treated as adults, and as a result, Pennsylvania has its first prison reserved for underage offenders. All the while he had little patience with his critics, from death penalty opponents to civil libertarians.

But Ridge's defining moment, insofar as his usefulness to George W. Bush is concerned, came during the Republican National

Convention in Philadelphia in the summer of 2000. The Republicans were gathering to anoint Bush as their savior against Al Gore, and wanted to be spared the sight of daily demonstrations in the streets that would be telecast worldwide. Ridge had the answer. As Angus Love, an attorney with the Pennsylvania Institutional Law Project, tells it:

> I was down there at the 2000 Republican Convention when the City of Brotherly Love was turned into a police state. Protest headquarters were pre-emptively raided by police on flimsy charges. Protest leaders were taken off the streets by plainclothes officers, South American-style. Almost all the charges against the 500 people who were arrested were eventually dropped. But the peace was kept. Bush the Second was anointed with barely a squeak from the unruly rabble. Who did we have to thank? None other than our new Homeland Security Czar. Get to know him, and you'll be unpleasantly surprised.

Ridge's use of a report from the wildly right-wing Malden Institute to justify the raid on the demonstrators was particularly unsettling. As Love put it, the think tank "used innuendo, lies and rumor in its propaganda-filled manifesto, suggesting that the global protest movement was funded by rubles smuggled out of the Soviet Union. The raid, prior to the protest, raised many troubling legal questions, most notably, prior restraint of First Amendment rights."

After his appointment as Homeland Security chief, Ridge sought unprecedented police powers. Asked by a reporter if we'd be living in a garrison state, Ridge shot back, "Get used to it."

So said the czar. However, throwing a blanket over civil freedoms does nothing to help Ridge's bloated bureaucracy thwart terrorists. It is a hit-and-miss game in any case—that is the nature of the beast. The point is made in the case of the would-be Millennial Bomber. Two weeks before the millennium, a Canadian named

Ahmed Ressam appeared unduly nervous to a U.S. Customs officer as he disembarked at Port Angeles, Washington, from a ferry coming from Victoria, British Columbia. A search of his rental car turned up the ingredients of a powerful bomb, and, after trying to flee, he was taken into custody. Ressam confessed that he intended to blow up the Los Angeles International Airport terminal two days before the millennium. He identified two other members of his terrorist cell, which was based in Montreal and supported itself through petty crime, but couldn't—or wouldn't—provide a link to al-Qaida. The case illustrates how random it is to block terrorists from entering the country. If Ressam had not become noticeably nervous and the Customs officer had not been extraordinarily observant, the Los Angeles air terminal would have been leveled. What makes this scenario doubly disturbing is that Ressam didn't have to risk smuggling the bomb ingredients into the United States—they can be easily procured here. For instance, ammonium nitrate, which when mixed with fuel oil can be a powerful explosive, is in common use as an agricultural fertilizer (Timothy McVeigh used it in the 1995 bombing of the Oklahoma City federal building, which took 168 lives). That is why the FBI has requested stores selling agricultural chemicals to report suspicious purchases.

The DHS also has a mission impossible in its responsibility for preventing the entry of possible terrorists and their weapons into the United States. Bogus identification papers documenting a "legend"—an innocent life story—are available on black markets all over the world. Watch lists are limited to known terrorist suspects, allowing the unknown a chance to enter. Illegal entry is not confined to border-crossing stations. There are thousands of miles of unpatrolled borders with Canada to the north and Mexico to the south over which drug traffickers and "coyotes"—smugglers of humans—have little difficulty in crossing. The narcotics control authorities have had only a modicum of success in interdicting contraband brought in by small airplanes, helicopters and boats. The American frontiers are porous, and there is no way to seal them short of erecting a Berlin Wall stretching from sea to sea.

The makings of a "dirty bomb" are also available domestically. When FBI agents took Jose Padilla into custody as he stepped off a commercial flight in Chicago, they had been tipped off by an al-Qaida captive in Pakistan that Padilla was on a mission to set off a dirty bomb. He certainly didn't bring one with him, so, if the tip wasn't a deception, he presumably would assemble one from components in the United States that he could lay his hands on.

A dirty bomb consists of a standard explosive such as dynamite that is packaged with a radioactive material that scatters when the bomb goes off. It kills or injures through the initial blast and by spreading radiation and contamination, hence the term "dirty." Although no dirty bomb attacks have ever been mounted, a measure of their potential can be gained from a 1987 leak of just three and a half ounces of a highly radioactive powder from an abandoned radiology machine in Brazil. Four people were killed, sixty hospitalized and thousands exposed to the radiation. John Pike, director of the Global Security Organization, characterized the damage from a dirty bomb: "You have long-term potential health hazards and you have longer-term psychological, social and political impacts that can go on for weeks, months, maybe years."

The radioactive materials for these devices—cesium, cobalt and indium isotopes—are widely employed in medical and industrial applications and are easy to come by. The materials are stored in thousands of hospitals, laboratories and factories across the land, often with little security. In April 2002, *ABC News* reported that

more than 1,500 radioactive devices have been lost, stolen or abandoned, and the federal government can account for only 660 of
them. It is an impossible task for Ridge's DHS to eliminate this
threat.

Chemical weapons likewise need not be smuggled in from
abroad—the chemicals can be obtained locally. The puzzle is how
to spread them in sufficient concentrations to be lethal. In the aftermath of 9/11, when it was discovered that a number of al-Qaida suspects had been taking flight training, there was alarm that they were
preparing to fly crop-dusting airplanes to spread toxic chemicals.
The FBI alerted flight academies and crop-dusting operators to report any suspicious contact. To attack a city with sarin, however, it
would be necessary to fly thousands of pounds back and forth over
populated areas. At that, the dilution factor would render it a not
very viable option. Amy Smithson, a chemical and biological weapons expert at the Henry Stimson Center in Washington, commented
to *Time*, October 1, 2001: "Any bozo can make a chemical agent in a
beaker, but producing tons and tons is difficult." The 1995 sarin
assault by the Aum Shinrikyo cult on the Tokyo subway, which is in
effect a closed container, shows the need for large quantities. The
cultists dropped plastic bags filled with sarin on a subway platform and pierced them with umbrella tips, releasing relatively small
quantities. At that, twelve people died. Aum Shinrikyo had tried to
manufacture sarin in bulk, hiring scientists and spending in the
neighborhood of $10 million, but failed. If a terrorist lab can figure
out how to produce it in sufficient quantity and deliver it—trouble.
There is also the possibility of introducing some other deadly gas
such as the nerve gas VX or cyanide into a closed area. Thirty years
ago, domestic terrorists belonging to the radical right-wing Minute-
men organization discussed the feasibility of injecting poison gas

into the air-conditioning system of the U.N. headquarters in New York. The DHS is challenged in coming up with effective counter-measures.

Biological warfare has been around since the Middle Ages, when armies besieging a city would catapult corpses infected with the Black Plague over the walls. Today the most feared germs are anthrax (a bacterium), which is not communicable, and smallpox (a virus), which is to a high degree. Both have high fatality rates. And both can be transported in vials. During the Cold War, the United States and the Soviet Union began developing anthrax as a biological weapon. Today, according to *Time* on October 1, 2001, "17 nations are believed to have biological weapons programs, many of which involve anthrax. Officially, the only sources of smallpox are small quantities in the labs of the Centers for Disease Control in Atlanta and at Vector in Koltsovo, Russia. But experts believe that Russia, Iraq and North Korea have all experimented with the virus and that significant secret stashes remain. Even more worrisome are reports that Russia used genetic engineering to try to make anthrax and smallpox more lethal and resistant to antibiotics and vaccines." The fear is that some of the Russian supply has fallen into the wrong hands.

The immediate thought would be to vaccinate each and every American against every possible germ-warfare agent. But the logistics of such a program are defeating, and the potential side effects serious. So far the smallpox shots have been given largely to the first responders—medical personnel, firemen, police. The only defense is early warning that a biological attack has taken place—putting hospitals and public health authorities on notice to report any signs of an outbreak so that it can be contained before turning into an epidemic.

More than thirty years ago, in an eerie foreshadowing of the 9/11 attacks, the writer John McPhee explored in a *Time* article with nuclear physicist Ted Taylor the question of whether the twin towers could be toppled with a small atomic bomb. They came to the conclusion that, positioned correctly, a nuclear device a tenth as powerful as the one dropped on Hiroshima could knock a tower into the Hudson River. But fabricating a small nuke would not be like assembling a toy in which the batteries are not included. The terrorists would first have to lay hands on enriched uranium, the most likely source of which would be the former Soviet Union. Although the United States assisted Russia with funding and scientists to account for and neutralize nuclear materials, it may have been a case of closing the barn door after the horse had already escaped. It is believed that bombmaking supplies are still available at the right price. Osama bin Laden reportedly has tried to buy uranium from the breakaway Soviet states, but his sources flummoxed him, offering instead low-grade reactor fuel and radioactive waste. Even if al-Qaida should succeed in acquiring uranium, there would remain a formidable challenge to fashion it into a nuke. Princeton University nuclear proliferation expert Frank von Hippel estimates it would take at least 150 pounds of uranium and hundreds of pounds of casing and machinery to make a nuke. "Nobody's going to be carrying a bomb around in a suitcase," he observes. Although it would be foolhardy to underestimate al-Qaida's capabilities, a more plausible scenario for a nuclear release would be an air or ground attack on a nuclear power plant using conventional explosives. Mindful of this, the Nuclear Regulatory Commission began staging commando-raid exercises on the plants even before 9/11. Disturbingly, some of the mock raids succeeded, in some cases resulting in a mock release of radiation exceeding that of Chernobyl.

The nation's airlines remain vulnerable despite the safeguards put in place by the DHS's Transportation Security Administration (TSA). The TSA replaced the private security firms that were handling the airport screening of passengers with its own personnel. The results have not been spectacular: Alarming quantities of knives, sharp instruments, and, yes, box cutters have passed through the screening posts. Media reporters have bypassed the security to show how it's done. A July 2002 survey by the TSA itself "found that fake guns, bombs, and other weapons got past security screeners almost one-fourth of the time."

That the system has more holes than Swiss cheese was shown in October 2003 by a North Carolina college student named Nathaniel Heatwole. At New Orleans and Houston airports, Southwest Airlines maintenance crews routinely checking behind lavatory wall panels found separate plastic bags containing box cutter blades, clay (simulating plastic explosives) and chlorine (simulating bomb-making chemicals) along with a note saying, "Look what I can do." The airline announced that notes in the bags of box cutters "indicated the items were intended to challenge the TSA checkpoint security procedures." When the FBI tracked down Heatwole, it turned out that was exactly what he had in mind. He was prosecuted, but he should have been awarded the Medal of Freedom for public service. But the TSA didn't go to school on the Heatwole experiment. "Amateur testing of our systems does not show us in any way our flaws," remarked Deputy Administrator Stephen McHale sourly. "We know where the vulnerabilities are and we are testing them. . . . This does not help."

The TSA has not been free from scandal. In June 2003 it acknowledged "firing more than 1,200 airport screeners—roughly 2 percent of its screener workforce—for providing false information on job applications, failing drug tests or having criminal records." Then a flap broke out when it was learned that TSA employees taking certification tests had been given the exact questions and answers in advance.

Robert Higgs, a senior fellow at The Independent Institute in Oakland, California, sees the program in Orwellian terms: "It routinely abases and humiliates the entire population, rendering us docile and compliant and thereby preparing us to play our assigned role in the police state that the Bush administration has been building relentlessly."

A very real threat to airliners is shoulder-fired surface-to-air missiles such as the Russian Strelas or SA-7s and American Stingers, thousands of which are in the hands of terrorists. In the 1980s the CIA armed the Taliban in Afghanistan with Stingers to shoot down Soviet helicopters; after the Soviet withdrawal it failed in its attempts to buy back the Stingers at a bonus price. James O'Halloran, editor of *Jane's Land-Based Air Defense* in England, told the *San Francisco Chronicle* on November 7, 2003, about the proliferation of SAMs: "There are literally hundreds of thousands of them in the world. Just about every country produces them now. You can run around all day with one on your shoulder and not get tired. And they're very, very cheap. That's what makes them the favorite of these [terrorist] organizations." In 2002 an Israeli charter jet taking off from an East African resort area narrowly missed being hit by a SAM. In October 2003 a DHL cargo jet was actually clipped by a SAM approaching the Baghdad airport, but the damage was not disastrous. The DHS's answer has been to try to secure the perimeters of major American airports, since the missiles must be fired at an aircraft after takeoff or before landing due to their limited range of accuracy. But the ring-around-the-airport theory was dealt a severe blow in August 2003 when three lost fishermen beached their boat at the end of JFK International Airport in New York and wandered undetected for a mile between runways.

It took Congress, acting under pressure from airline pilots, to put into action the surest countermeasure, an automatic device that can detect a heat-seeking missile and deflect it. Two years after 9/11, Congress passed a law requiring U.S. airlines to spend $100,000 per device to install it on all new aircraft. Eventually, aircraft already in service will be retrofitted with the device. Eventually. Tom Ridge seemed to have no sense of urgency in getting this done, which amounted to an invitation to tragedy.

It is perhaps a gauge of Ridge's competency that he is most remembered for his February 2003 "duct tape" recommendation. In line with his effort to acquaint Americans with how to protect themselves in the event of a terrorist strike—there were precious few realistic tips—Ridge suggested that citizens buy plastic sheeting and tape it to seal an "internal room" in their homes to thwart a biological or chemical assault. The result was a run on plastic sheeting and duct tape at such home improvement stores as Home Depot and Lowe's while critics howled in derision (what if you're not home?). Ridge insisted that the countermeasure was practical, indirectly blaming Democrats for the belittling. He took the hint, however, and in November 2003 ballyhooed a system called Biowatch, installed in thirty-one cities across the nation. This is a sensor network that constantly monitors the air for biological pathogens. But Biowatch, too, was not immune from criticism that it might induce a false sense of security. It doesn't detect small releases that could sicken thousands, doesn't monitor indoor venues such as sports arenas, and lets too many hours pass between a possible attack and the testing of air samples. "Unless it is a major atmospheric release of large quantities of materials," appraised Calvin Chue, a research scientist at Johns Hopkins University, for the Associated Press on November 14, 2003, "I do not think it would be hard at all for Biowatch to miss an attack."

Yet Tom Ridge barnstormed the country propagating his message that the DHS has made America a more secure place. On July 23, 2003, for example, he told the Commonwealth Club of San Francisco that the country is safer now than before 9/11, a rash pronouncement. At the same time, he has kept up a steady drumbeat of doomsday warnings, using his sophomoric color code called the Homeland Security Advisory System: Red is for severe risk of attack; orange high; yellow elevated; blue guarded; and green low. While this may be of some value to police and other first responders, it is only bewildering to the citizenry, since the warnings are usually nonspecific. When the code jumps from blue to orange, what measures should be taken? Don't cross the Golden Gate Bridge? Don't attend a football game at Giants Stadium? Stay indoors? Walk down the street backwards? The warnings are usually based on information from newly captured al-Qaida operatives overseas, another audiotape from Osama bin Laden, or a sharp increase in electronic signals traffic attributed to al-Qaida. The problem is that the information can just as easily be disinformation designed to keep America's anxieties at a high level.

Ironically, keeping Americans terrorized is a strategy George Bush shares with bin Laden. It is the capstone of his reelection campaign. In November 2003, one full year before Election 2004, television spots started airing Bush in his State of the Union address the previous January issuing a dire warning: "It would take one vial, one canister, one crate slipped into this country to bring a day of horror like none we have ever known." The aim is to have Americans running scared while Bush is running for reelection, portraying him as the indispensable leader in the war on terrorism.

If anything, Bush is a security risk precisely because his every move is politically calculated. Creating the biggest—and most inflexible—bureaucracy in government may look impressive, and putting a hidebound politician in charge of it might be the political thing to do. But even if it was sleeker, DHS's chances of averting another Big One are slim to nonexistent. It is necessary to dig out the terrorist cells on homeland soil, and that operational assignment goes to the FBI. Unfortunately, the Bureau has little conception of the cunning and deception of the enemy it is facing. In an article entitled "Red Alert" for *National Review Online* on November 20, 2002, Mark Riebling put it in perspective:

> That al Qaeda is not highly sophisticated has been the working assumption of the FBI since bin Laden came to its attention in 1993, after the first World Trade Center bombing. This downplaying seems to be a corollary of the idea that al Qaeda lacks state sponsorship, and is, therefore, an amorphous, ad-hoc group, without any strict doctrine or formal structure. That view has survived at the bureau even after 9/11. The hijackers were not "a cohesive group," one FBI agent told Seymour Hersh, late last year, but just "a bunch of guys who got together . . . [like] a pickup basketball team." They were not skilled so much as they were "simply lucky."

Like a pickup basketball team. That kind of simplistic reasoning is why I have long advocated that the FBI's counterintelligence division be spun off from what is quintessentially a law enforcement outfit and staffed with specialists every bit as sophisticated as the enemy. Riebling sees al-Qaida as more than an intellectual match for the FBI: "The 9/11 attacks were nothing if not brilliantly planned and executed. How the terrorists orchestrated such an elaborate and unprecedented operation; how they sluiced tens of thousands of dollars, and moved and cocooned nearly two dozen men, across several continents, and around the U.S., over several years, without detection—these questions ought to haunt us. The simplest and the best answer, to my mind, is that given by former CIA officer Robert Baer: 'The people who planned this attack are good. Very good.'"

They are good enough to have outsmarted the FBI on 9/11. And it augurs a reoccurrence because Bush didn't see 9/11 as a wake-up call. Shaking up the FBI was not on his political agenda. But it should have been on his security list. The stakes are simply too high to leave bad enough alone.

7

WHY THE FBI
FLUNKED ITS TERROR TEST

It was a matter of multiple missed signals, of opportunities lost. For
more than two years, a large al-Qaida cell hid in plain sight while
conspiring to pull off the 9/11 attacks. The members took flying lessons, used Visa cards for travel and purchases, rented Mail Boxes
Etc. boxes as dead drops, sometimes communicating in code. Clues
as to what was stirring kept cropping up. In early 2001 in the New
York trial of four people indicted for the 1998 deadly bombings of
American embassies in Kenya and Tanzania there was testimony,
in exchange for a plea bargain, that two men connected to Osama
bin Laden were taking pilot training in Oklahoma and Texas. Not
long afterward an alert Arizona FBI agent signaled headquarters
that Middle Eastern men were enrolled in a local flight school, but
his recommendation that a nationwide survey be conducted was
ignored. In early August a Minnesota flight academy instructor reported to the FBI that a man named Zacarias Moussaoui proffered
cash to learn how to fly a jumbo jet but didn't need to know how to
land it; instead of clamping a physical and electronic surveillance

on Moussaoui to learn his movements and identify other members of his cell, which conceivably might have led to Mohammed Atta, the ringleader, agents summarily arrested him. On August 6, as the clock was ticking, President Bush received a CIA briefing while on vacation at his Texas ranch that an al-Qaida plot was in the works to take over civilian airliners in flight and crash them into buildings. At the same time, the CIA belatedly notified the Bureau that two men implicated in the October 2000 bombing of the USS *Cole* in Yemen, Khalid al-Midhar and Nawaq Alhamzi, had triggered its watch list by reentering the United States. Settled down in San Diego, listed in the phone book, the pair went unlocated until 9/11, when they crashed American Airlines Flight 77 into the Pentagon.

Despite this prima facie evidence that the FBI is woefully inadequate at processing the information it collects, leaving the nation vulnerable to another Big One, and another after that, George W. Bush did not fundamentally revamp the FBI. It was practically business as usual. He threw millions of more dollars at his FBI chief, Robert Mueller, authorizing him to hire nine hundred more agents. In turn, Mueller announced he was reassigning hundreds of agents working white-collar crime and bank robberies to the National Security Division to meet the contemporary challenge of terrorism. It was the same old Bureau numbers game: More is better. The "reforms" were superficial, akin to rearranging the deck chairs on the *Titanic*. Even Mueller was moved to admit he could not guarantee that the FBI, with its new priority, could avert every terrorist act. This was not what Bush wanted to hear, and Mueller corrected himself: The FBI was now up to speed, perfectly capable of defending the nation against terrorism.

Wrong. There is no reason to believe that the FBI is now equipped to thwart terrorism when it wasn't before 9/11. And the risk has greatly increased, thanks to Bush's Iraq diversion, which gave al-Qaida and its allies breathing room and time to regroup and expand. From hiding, Osama bin Laden recently prophesied that another strike at America, one even exceeding 9/11 in scope, would happen soon. It isn't a question of if, but when. The 9/11 attacks came six years after the idea was conceived, but it is anybody's guess as to what projects may already be in an advanced stage. There is some indication from captured al-Qaida foot soldiers that a second wave of attacks was scheduled immediately after 9/11 but called off for unknown reasons. There is also the possibility that the "second wave" was actually carried out in the form of the anthrax cases in which the deadly powder was distributed through the postal system and left five people dead. This was definitely not a copycat caper, because the perpetrator had put the letters in the mail before a latency period for weaponized anthrax expired.

Primary responsibility for defending the home front is vested in the FBI, while the CIA is charged with operating overseas. The turf chalk lines were drawn by the Delimitations Agreement of 1947, after the FBI's ambitious director, J. Edgar Hoover, pushed to take over foreign intelligence as well. The G-men, as Hoover's minions were nicknamed—"Don't shoot, G-men," George "Machine Gun" Kelly had cried out when cornered by FBI agents—had earned a reputation as gangbusters par excellence by knocking off the John Dillingers and Pretty Boy Floyds who were pulling off bank robberies and kidnappings throughout the Midwest. During World War II, President Franklin Delano Roosevelt capitalized on Hoover's fame by tasking him with rooting out German and Japanese spies in America. The Bureau did a commendable job, although its accomplishments were often more a matter of public relations wizardry than brilliant sleuthing.

The case of the eight German saboteurs landed by submarine is the paradigm, cited by John Ashcroft today as precedent for trying suspects in secret military tribunals. As I recounted in *Hoover's FBI*, published in 1970, the official story was a piece of wartime propaganda designed to instill public confidence in the Bureau's prowess in protecting the home front. On the morning of June 13, 1942, eight men trained in demolition techniques in Germany slipped ashore from a U-boat near Amagansett, Long Island, and another sub on the Florida coast, then dispersed according to plan. Their eventual targets were a huge aluminum plant, Ohio River locks, and key railroad facilities. Sixteen days later newspaper headlines blazed: "FBI CAPTURES EIGHT GERMAN SABOTEURS LANDED BY SUBS." The accounts heaped praise on the FBI, telling how G-men started with the clue of German cigarettes that several of the men left behind as they rode trains into New York City and hunted them down.

The story was cut from whole cloth. After the war, New York *Daily News* reporter John O'Donnell wrote an article taglined: "Truth Will Out! Great Spy Hunt Exploded!" The article disclosed that President Harry Truman's attorney general, Tom Clark, had decided the time had come to open up the files of the secret trial of the eight saboteurs. "All were in the custody of the FBI within a fortnight of the landings," O'Donnell revealed. "Within sixty days six had been executed. Two, George Dasch and Ernst Burger, are in the Atlanta Penitentiary—Dasch serving a 30-year sentence, Burger life." O'Donnell went on: "The private files now made public by the Attorney General reveal that Dasch and Burger were haters of the Hitler regime, left Germany with the real saboteurs with the determination to expose the plot immediately on arrival, phoned the FBI headquarters in New York immediately on their secret arrival, went to Hoover's Washington office at once, poured out the

full story of the plot and the tale of how they had led the real saboteurs into the trap. Now this, of course, spoiled the carefully nursed
official story which poured all credit for the outstanding and sensational capture on the FBI and gave full credit to the brilliance, skill,
and scientific training of Director Hoover's outfit."

O'Donnell told how Hoover, after he got wind that *Newsweek*
was about to break the true story, protested vigorously to Tom Clark.
Intimidated, Clark called *Newsweek*, admitted that what they had
was totally accurate, but pleaded, "Hoover wants to make some
changes." When the *Newsweek* correspondent, John U. Terrell, refused to make changes, O'Donnell wrote, "Department of Justice
experts stayed up all night, whipped up their version, and slapped it
out to meet *Newsweek* publication — in a version designed to keep
up the public prestige of Hoover and the FBI."

A postscript was added in 1959 when George Dasch, one of the
defecting saboteurs who had been sneaked back to Germany, cor-
roborated the O'Donnell exposure in a thin volume called *Eight
Spies Against America*, which received meager distribution. Dasch
related that the New York FBI office didn't believe his account of
being landed by submarine, and when he showed up at headquarters in Washington, officials at first scoffed at his story. It was only
when he spilled out some $80,000 in cash the Germans had given
him that they decided to check it out. Since he knew where the
rendezvous were to be made, it was a simple matter for the FBI to
make the roundup. Dasch, who before the war had lived for a time
in New York and expected to be treated as an American hero for
undoubtedly saving many lives, said he was told he would have to
stand trial with his compatriots in order to fool the Germans, but
that within six months, after a sham conviction, he would be fully
exonerated and freed. Instead, he was sentenced to thirty years. At

the end of the closed military trial, Dasch wrote, he came face to face with Hoover and tried to plead with him:

> He continued on, ignoring me. Again I cried out, this time louder than before: "Mr. Hoover, aren't you really ashamed of yourself?"
>
> An FBI agent walking nearby struck me on the face, sending me sprawling on the floor. One of the army guards helped me to my feet, and through the tears brought on by the hot sting of the agent's hand, I saw the Chief disappear down the hall, seemingly surrounded by an impregnable wall of justice and strength.

At war's end, President Harry Truman decided, based on the exploits of the Office of Strategic Services in Europe, that the United States needed an overseas intelligence capacity even in peacetime. Hoover, citing his apparent success in combating Axis spies at home and in South America, argued that his FBI should take over the function. But Truman was leery of Hoover, feeling he had too much power to begin with, and created the CIA instead. The FBI chief never got over this blow to his formidable ego—he touched off the turf wars between the Bureau and the Agency that still go on. I recall that in the early 1960s when I was an FBI agent specializing in counterintelligence against the Soviets, I was admonished by my field supervisor in Seattle, Julius Matson, who cracked a Japanese code during the war, not to pass on information that might be of interest to the CIA directly to its local office. Any such data had to be memoed to Bureau headquarters in Washington, where a decision was made whether or not the Agency should be notified. Of course, by the time it passed through this bureaucratic maze it might be stale.

It was while doing this stint in Seattle that I realized counterintelligence was not one of Hoover's top priorities. Only rarely did it produce headlines, the idea being to prevent the loss of state secrets by quietly neutralizing the adversary's agents. But I had welcomed the intellectual challenge, and volunteered for the assignment. I quickly learned that not all of my Squad Five colleagues shared my enthusiasm. Julius Matson was eminently qualified for this type of work but was burdened with supervising criminal cases as well. Another seasoned agent, Bert Zander, knew his stuff but bitched about the Espionage Desk managers in Washington as being models of inertia. One agent tended to his personal real estate investments more than to the counterspy business, while another simply took up space while watching the clock. There was no special training for this specialized field, no comprehensive Manual of Instructions. I plunged right in by interviewing Soviet-bloc emigrés, and traveling to Vancouver, Canada, combing through Canadian Pacific steamship manifests from the 1930s looking for "illegals" that might have entered from the Far East. The "dark side" of the FBI was in fact pure drudgery, not at all like the fast pace of criminal pursuit I was used to.

One case that I handled illustrated how exasperating counterintelligence could be—and why Hoover assigned it such low priority. From monitoring the Soviet Embassy in Mexico City, which was the Western Hemisphere nerve center for the KGB, we identified a "sleeper agent" who was living in the Ballard section of Seattle. He and his wife owned a home in a middle-class neighborhood, both were employed, and they had a son in college. On the surface a typical American family. But we knew that he was awaiting a phone call that would activate him in that defense-industry-rich city, so I installed a wiretap on his home phone. After a period during which no call came, the FBI laboratory instructed me to yank the wiretap and install a bug (listening device). The wiretap allotment, it seemed, was needed to balance the books for Hoover's annual trek to Capitol Hill, during which he would testify that nationwide there were only one hundred or so wiretaps in service, all properly authorized by the attorney general in national security cases. What he didn't mention was the rampant illegal bugging, which he was bootlegging. So I had to break-and-enter to install a bug, fracturing the Bill of Rights and the state of Washington criminal code, and risk blowing the whole operation to boot. Today, under the Foreign Intelligence Surveillance Act of 1978, wiretapping, bugging and break-ins are legal with the issuance of a warrant by a secret court.

Another impediment to success in the counterintelligence field was the lack of ethnic diversity among the agents. Practically all were Caucasian, recruited for the most part from Catholic and Mormon schools and Southern universities, producing a cookie-cutter G-man (there were no women agents while Hoover lived). There was a cultural divide between us and our adversaries. I recall an occasion when the State Department notified the Bureau that three military attaches to the Soviet Embassy in Washington had been given permission to visit Seattle. It was axiomatic that military attaches were spies, and there were certain sensitive zones in the area that were off-limits. We were prepared for them. When they arrived in town, the good people at Hertz put them in a rental car that we had outfitted with a "bumper beeper" tracking device. Then the management at the Benjamin Franklin Hotel steered them to a room I had pre-bugged. To our surprise, they suddenly decided to take off for parts unknown. We rushed for our own cars and discreetly tailed them. They drove leisurely to Bellingham, near the Canadian border, where they checked into a small hotel and bought oranges and tins of sardines at a grocery next door. The other agents assumed the Russians bought the oranges and sardines for a night snack in their room—no one would eat sardines for breakfast—and would have an American breakfast in the hotel's coffee shop. But I knew that Russians would indeed eat sardines for breakfast. So in the morning, while my two colleagues enjoyed breakfast in the coffee shop while waiting for the Russians to show up, I sat in my car ready to take up the surveillance. And sure enough, the Russians rushed right through the lobby, hopped into their car and sped south. I was able to keep up with them as they turned west and pulled up under the flight path of the Whidbey Island Naval Air Station, home base to P2V electronic spy planes patrolling off the Far East coast of the Soviet Union, and forbidden territory for them. When they spotted me in my trademark Bureau Ford, they put away their cameras and drove slowly back to Seattle.

It was instances like this that convinced me that the FBI should stick to its criminal legacy and leave the more sophisticated field of counterintelligence to another agency especially devoted to it. In *Hoover's FBI*, I compared the type of agent recruited by the FBI with that of the CIA, which proselytized exclusively for intelligence work: "The type of man who would make the best counterspy would never pass FBI muster or flourish in its anti-intellectual environment. Hoover might look down his nose at the 'Harvard Yard liberals' and somewhat off-beat types employed by the CIA, but in the final analysis the machine-gun mentality didn't crack spy rings."

I pointed out the clash of cultures: Bureau officials disdainfully alluded to the CIA director as "Princeton Ought-Ought" and his brain trust as "high-domed theoreticians," while the CIA hierarchy looked down its nose at Hoover as "that cop." The degree of difference was nicely expressed by Kim Philby, a 1950s British diplomat in Washington who liaised with FBI and CIA agents in the course of his duties. "FBI agents were whiskey-drinkers, with beer for light refreshment," said Philby, who turned out to be a Soviet double agent. "By contrast, CIA men flaunted cosmopolitan postures. They would discuss absinthe, and serve Burgundy above room temperature."

In a paper delivered to the 1971 Princeton Conference on the FBI sponsored by the university's Woodrow Wilson School of Public Affairs (and published in *Investigating the FBI*), I expanded on the theme:

> This cop-versus-intellectual distinction points up another FBI lack in the counterespionage field. Hoover's views were essentially those of a cop—he oversimplified and failed to comprehend nuances and subtleties. In my experience, most FBI agents are not only unsuited to counterespionage, they don't want it. The Bureau made its mark early in criminal detection, and the agency's recruiting and training programs are heavily loaded in that direction. Nor did Hoover tolerate the kind of unorthodox, semi-Bohemian, perhaps long-haired individual who traditionally has made the best counterspy. Such types are, however, welcomed by the CIA.
>
> The imperative is clear. The FBI should be divested of its counterespionage responsibilities, which are incompatible with the Bureau's essentially criminal investigative nature. However, I would not recommend that they be turned over to the CIA; that agency is already too large and without effective control. Rather, create a separate division within the Department of Justice that will function under the statutory authority of the Espionage Act and National Security Act. Staff it with imaginative men, and appoint a director willing to operate in obscurity. Call it descriptively the Division of Counterespionage (DCE). And let there be no television series *The DCE*. Counterespionage is best conducted backstage, without theatrics.

There was international precedent for divorcing the two functions, I argued: "The United States is the only major power vesting counterespionage and criminal responsibilities under one roof."

It was precisely because of glowing media treatment of the Bureau—the long-running television series *The FBI*, starring Efrem

Zimbalist as Inspector Erskine, which was subject to content control by the Bureau, is a prime example—that the organization was resistant to change. Over the decades the more things have changed, the more they stayed the same. The Hoover legacy lives on, the dynamics untouched. The Bureau remains arrogant, insular, hardly a model of diversity, rigidly conservative, risk-adverse, prone to cover-up. Rare is the agent who dares to think outside the box; the disciplinary ax will fall. In November 2003, the Department of Justice inspector general, Glenn Fine, issued a report of investigation finding that senior FBI managers got away with inappropriate sexual behavior and questionable racial and sexual comments, while ordinary agents were given harsh sanctions for similar offenses. One of the cases cited in the report involved a deputy assistant director— one of the highest-ranking officials—who allegedly had sex with two subordinates, contacted witnesses in an attempt to obstruct an internal probe, and allowed two prostitutes to accompany him from a nightclub to his hotel during a training trip. By contrast, a low-level agent who made an off-color joke about talk show host Oprah Winfrey's weight at a training class was handed a formal letter of censure, which would impede his career advancement. This double standard was nothing new. At the 1971 Princeton Conference I reported that the Bureau's reputation for incorruptibility was preserved by cover-ups. An example:

> One high-ranking official is an alcoholic, and has been involved in many drunken scenes, including one in Toots Shor's in New York City and others on airline flights and in many field offices. On one occasion he demanded that two prostitutes be provided by the Chicago office. He also forced the Chicago FBI to buy him an engine for his personal boat at a cost of about $1,000. This was covered by phony vouchers in the office fund for confidential informants.

The FBI's responsibility for counterespionage has in recent years been expanded by jurisdiction over counterterrorism within U.S. borders, and it doesn't merit passing grades. The chronicle can be said to start with the first World Trade Center bombing in New York in 1993, which cost six lives and over a thousand injuries. Federal Bureau of Alcohol, Tobacco & Firearms (ATF) agents, sifting through the debris, found the nameplate of the blasted van that had been driven into the basement and traced the serial number to a Ryder rental agency in New Jersey. The FBI took over from there, determining that the van had been rented in his name by a follower of the radical blind Muslim cleric, Sheikh Omar Abdul Rahman. Rahman and nine members of his cell were convicted, with the FBI blowing them off as a loose group of fundamentalists.

What is scary, however, is the story behind the story of how the Bureau could have prevented the disaster in the first place had it not been internally conflicted. According to reporter Ralph Blumenthal in the *New York Times* on October 28, 1993, an informant named Emad Salem penetrated the cell and was actually helping construct the bomb. The scheme called for Salem to foil the bombing by substituting harmless powder for the explosive. But an FBI supervisor, Salem complained, "came and messed it up," insisting that he blow his cover by testifying. The *Times* account elaborated that "Salem wanted to complain to FBI headquarters in Washington about the Bureau's failure to stop the bombing, but was dissuaded by an agent identified as John Anticev." When Blumenthal called a headquarters agent, Nancy Floyd, she commiserated with the Manhattan agents in their reluctance to brief Washington. "Well, of course not," she said, "because they don't want to get their butts chewed." To cavalierly wave off such conduct is inexcusable. But what Floyd may not have known was that forensic scientists in their crime scene investigation found that one tower was supposed to topple on the other, releasing a cloud of cyanide gas that would kill thousands. One didn't need a crystal ball to realize that al-Qaida would be back some day with enough explosive power to do the job.

As it turned out, dismissing Sheikh Rahman's cell as an isolated one was an egregious mistake that might have cost hundreds of lives. One key operative in the bombing, Ramzi Yousef, who was related to Osama bin Laden's top lieutenant Abu Zubaydah, slipped away before he could be identified. In January 1995, the Philippine National Police notified the FBI that Yousef had fled the Josefa apartments in Manila after chemicals he was mixing ignited. He left behind evidence that he and cell members planned to blow up eleven American airliners in Asian skies in a one-day spectacular. Also on the agenda, a cell member confessed, was to suicide dive a hijacked airliner into CIA headquarters in Virginia. Eventually captured by Pakistani authorities, Yousef was returned to New York and convicted of the World Trade Center bombing. So more than six years before 9/11, the FBI knew that hijacking civilian airliners and converting them to flying bombs crashing into symbolic targets was being given high priority by al-Qaida.

The Bureau culture, however, is so embedded that it is institutionally incapable of changing, remaining a dinosaur in an age of new challenges. No case better illustrates the point than that of Robert Hanssen, an FBI counterintelligence specialist who in early 2001 was unmasked as a Russian spy. The FBI had its own Hall of Shame. In 1984 Richard W. Miller, a Bible-reading California agent, traded classified documents to a female Soviet spy for oral sex and money (he was tripped up through his own clumsiness). Beginning in 1987, New York agent Earl E. Pitts sold sensitive data to the Soviets for several years (he was finally turned in by his wife). Recently, in April 2003, veteran Los Angeles agent James J. Smith was charged with having "a long sexual relationship" with double agent Katrina Leung, which resulted in the transmission of counterespionage secrets to China.

What sets apart the Hanssen case was how long it went on, despite a series of neon signs pointing to him as the mole the Bureau knew was in its midst. For twenty years Hanssen fitfully delivered classified documents to the KGB and its successor agency, the SVR, for large bundles of cash left in dead drops. For years, while the national security was compromised time and time again, the Bureau ignored Hanssen's unauthorized hacking of computers and the suspicions of one of his colleagues to focus exclusively on a senior CIA agent named Brian Kelly. It was not until 2001 that the SVR, with Hanssen's usefulness at an end, dumped him by routing his Russian personnel file to the FBI through back channels. But Kelly's CIA career was in ruins. An FBI spokesman questioned by CBS's 60 Minutes refused to apologize. The Bureau had not been wrong, he said, it just had not been right. But Department of Justice Inspector General Michael Bromwich had the last word: "Inadequate controls over highly classified information and weak screening and monitoring of employees."

The 1999 Wen Ho Lee case at the Los Alamos National Laboratory at Santa Fe, New Mexico, was an example of sheer ineptitude. Suspicious that Lee, a scientist at the lab, might have passed on classified information to Chinese colleagues at scientific meetings, the FBI slogged along indeterminably. The lead agent on the case was a local who pursued the investigation between handling bank robberies and crimes on an Indian reservation. Others entered the picture and left. With practically no evidence except that he was careless with computer security, Lee was jailed. At a bail hearing, agent Robert Messemer admitted that he had made an "honest mistake" in reporting earlier that Lee had made an incriminating statement. In his *The Bureau*, Ronald Kessler wrote: "The admission was devastating. The fact that an agent could give false testimony in such an important case showed how far the bureau had fallen since the days of [Director] William Webster. In 1985 alone, the FBI under Webster arrested eleven major spies without a single claim that rights had been violated or that the FBI had acted improperly." Complaining that he had been "led astray" by the executive branch, Judge James A. Parker freed Lee, saying his jailing "embarrassed our entire nation and each of us who is a citizen of it." Randy I. Bellows, a federal prosecutor who looked into the affair, commented: "This investigation was a paradigm of how not to manage a counter-intelligence case." He might have added that it was also a paradigm of what happens when a criminal investigator is assigned a counter-intelligence case.

The tragedy of 9/11 is that the FBI had information that, if properly followed up, might have identified the Atta cell and averted the attacks. In the late 1990s al-Qaida began inserting operatives into the United States to learn to fly. The pattern went undetected until June 2001, three months before 9/11, when an alert Phoenix agent, Kenneth Williams, directed a memo to headquarters reporting that there were a number of flight students in his area who might be al-Qaida. There was some assumption that they might be intending to use crop-dusting planes to spray chemical toxins. Williams recommended that a nationwide survey be conducted. His memo would end up in the in-basket of David Frasca, supervisor of the Radical Fundamentalist Unit. Nothing was done. Frasca later claimed he had not seen the memo until after 9/11.

A considerably more specific clue as to what was shaping up came in the form of a phone call on August 14, almost a month before 9/11, from a Minneapolis flight academy instructor to the local FBI field office. The call was taken by David Rapp, a counterterrorism specialist. In an urgent tone, the instructor reported that he had a foreign student named Zacarias Moussaoui who wanted to learn how to fly a Boeing 747 but didn't need to know, in the interest of time, how to take off and land. The instructor was convinced that Moussaoui intended to convert an airliner into a flying bomb. Rapp agreed, and urgently signaled the same supervisor, Frasca, and others at headquarters, but the response was that there was "no proof" to justify a search warrant for Moussaoui's laptop computer. No proof? The mission seems to have been lost in lawyerly doublespeak within a bureaucracy noted for its aversion to risk. Counterintelligence protocol calls for clamping physical and electronic surveillance on a subject to find out who he is in contact with, the aim being to identify other members of the cell before neutralizing it. Even when French intelligence advised that Moussaoui was on their list of terrorists—he was a French national—headquarters didn't concede that legally that made him an international terrorist. So Rapp and the Minneapolis agents were forced to handle the case in criminal fashion, arresting him in his hotel room for an immigration violation. Still having no permission from Washington, they didn't search his computer. Unaccountably, they had a perfect legal right to search it, as well as everything in the room, incidental to his arrest—but didn't. So on 9/11 Moussaoui sat in jail, his cell comrades unidentified.

On May 23, 2002, after President Bush and Robert Mueller had made only patchwork reforms to the FBI's National Security Division, a senior agent/legal counsel of the Minneapolis office who was having night sweats over the Moussaoui blunder blew the whistle. In a blunt letter to the FBI director, Colleen Rowley addressed his contention that the FBI had no advance warning of the 9/11 plot. She wrote: "I think your statements demonstrate a rush to judgment to protect the FBI at all costs. . . . FBI headquarters is staffed with a number of short-term careerists . . . there is an unevenness in competency. . . . The ranks of FBI management are filled with many who were failures as street agents." Rowley averred that if the Moussaoui matter had been handled competently, "we might have gotten lucky" and averted the 9/11 attacks. She warned that without radical change, it would be déjà vu all over again.

Mueller reacted with fury, trying to hide her memo by classifying it. But Rowley had sent a copy to *Time* magazine, which courageously published it. So Mueller sent a message to others who might be tempted to blow the whistle by promoting David Frasca, while leaving Rowley in a career limbo. He continued to stonewall accountability when Chicago agent Robert Wright, who had tried to cut off the Saudi money trail leading to al-Qaida, went public with the charge that the headquarters International Terrorism Unit had obstructed his investigation, thus acting as a "spectator" while thousands died. Wright had prepared a lengthy manuscript detailing the money trail and obstruction, but Mueller blocked Congress from seeing it on the pretext that it might be used at a grand jury (which has never been convened). Keeping the lid on was a Mueller trait. When he was U.S. Attorney in San Francisco, he told the press: "Call me any time, even at home. And I'll give you the same 'no comment.'" He fit right in with an administration with an unprecedented penchant for secrecy.

The FBI's post-9/11 record in ferreting out terrorist cells hardly is reassuring. In fact, "ferreting" is the wrong verb—there were two instances, both the result of tips. One came from Khalid Sheikh

Mohammed, the top-echelon bin Laden operative captured by the Pakistanis. U.S. investigators believed he was in a position to give up bin Laden himself, which didn't happen. But along with naming the Golden Gate Bridge as a target, which wasn't exactly a secret, he gave up a Chicago street thug named Jose Padilla who had converted to Islam and attended an al-Qaida training camp in Pakistan. After he returned home, Padilla supposedly was going to make a "dirty bomb," one that spews radiological waste upon detonation, out of materials obtainable in the United States. He was arrested in May 2002 after he stepped off a plane in Chicago by FBI agents who chose not to tail him to see who he might contact out of fear they would lose him. Bereft of sufficient evidence to file charges, the Justice Department held him for the statutory time allowed, then declared him an "enemy combatant" and consigned him to a military prison, where he could be held incommunicado indefinitely. Zubaydah may well have considered Padilla a "throwaway," a valueless, low-level operative sacrificed to lend the appearance of cooperation.

In September 2002, FBI agents, in what the Bush administration hailed as a major victory in the war on terrorism, swooped down on Lackawanna, New York, a suburb of Buffalo, and arrested five local residents of Yemeni descent. At a press conference the local FBI agent in charge, Peter Ahearn, flanked by Republican Governor George Pataki, announced that his agents had broken up a terrorist "sleeper cell," although he admitted that no weapons were found and there was no evidence that the suspects were planning any specific terrorist acts. The entire case, it turned out, rested on information received from a tipster acquaintance of one of the suspects that in the summer of 2001 they made a pilgrimage to Pakistan to study Islam and, while there, crossed the border into Afghanistan to visit an al-Qaida camp where they "heard" Osama bin Laden speak. That was it. Rather than being a threat to the republic, they appeared to have been guilty of being in the wrong place at the wrong time. It also developed, according to a federal prosecutor, that the FBI investigation began before 9/11, raising the question of why, if they were truly a serious threat, they weren't detained in the wake of the attacks instead of a year later. At that, they were not charged with plotting terrorism but with "material support"—the side trip to an al-Qaida camp—to which they pleaded guilty. The whole affair seems to have been staged to make it seem there was material progress in the war on terrorism at home.

In the aftermath of the FBI's monumental failure to prevent the 9/11 attacks, sentiment in Congress grew to replace the National Security Division with a new, totally separate outfit tentatively called the Homeland Intelligence Agency (HIA). The proposal implicitly recognized that the FBI with its emphasis on criminal prosecution, cumbersome bureaucracy and culture of arrogance and cover-up was hopelessly overmatched by its terrorist adversaries. The new agency, its proponents argued, might be modeled after Britain's MI5, which concentrates on domestic counterintelligence to the exclusion of any criminal jurisdiction. On its Web site, MI5 defined its approach: "Over time, we try to obtain detailed knowledge about target organizations, their key personalities, infrastructure, plans and capabilities." MI5 has a reputation for quick development of intelligence and nimbleness in acting on it. Its effectiveness was illustrated in January 2003 when it learned that an al-Qaida cell housed in a London apartment possessed the deadly toxic ricin, intending to introduce it into the subway system. MI5, which operates in the dark, routinely called upon the local police to make the arrests—in contrast to the FBI, which craves publicity and makes its own arrests. In fact, the exchange of information between the FBI and local police has always been a one-way street in which the police feel used. One district attorney investigator with whom I talked put it this way: "FBI agents won't help until they get clearance from Washington, which takes time. Then they are apt to blow the surveillance and otherwise mess up. But they will hog the credit if the case turns out successful."

In October 2002, with the push for a Homeland Intelligence Agency gathering speed, the *Telegraph* of London disclosed that U.S. officials were contemplating the creation of a new organization designed along the lines of MI5 because "the FBI's 'police' culture is so entrenched that it cannot be transformed into an effective intelligence agency." With the heat on, George Bush dispatched Tom Ridge to meet with MI5 officials—to torpedo the idea of an American equivalent, as it turned out. Interviewed upon his return by George Stephanopoulos on *This Week*, Ridge complained: "I think it unfortunate my trip to England was misinterpreted. We went over there to learn a lot of lessons. Their MI5 is certainly different from anything we do here, and I suspect different from anything we would want to have done in this country." The reference was to the broad surveillance powers MI5 possesses—intercepting communications, eavesdropping and using informants and moles to infiltrate suspected terrorist groups. The inference was that forming an independent counterintelligence agency on the MI5 model would pose a serious threat to civil liberties. It is difficult to imagine how Ridge could keep a straight face knowing that the FBI already had powers surpassing those of MI5 under the Foreign Intelligence Surveillance Act and the USA Patriot Act.

But if Bush thought he had finessed the issue, he was mistaken. In February 2003 Senator John Edwards, a member of the Intelligence Committee, introduced legislation to create a Homeland Intelligence Agency "to replace FBI units that failed to uncover the September 11 terrorists and still cannot find suspected al Qaeda operatives in the United States." Edwards stated that while the FBI is a crack criminal investigative outfit, the 9/11 attacks "showed how it has failed as an intelligence gathering agency." He quoted former CIA General Counsel Jeffrey Smith: "Intelligence and law enforcement are such fundamentally different functions that they should not be performed in the same agency." Noting that Director Mueller had assumed that there were al-Qaida sleeper cells in the country, Edwards termed his "corrective measures" too little and too late. And Edwards wisely placed safeguards in the legislation restricting HIA's domestic spying. But the Bush administration strongly opposed the bill—Mueller called it "a step backwards in the war on terrorism"—and it remains bottled up in committee.

In July 2003 the Joint House-Senate Intelligence Committee issued a report pointing out the FBI and CIA's institutional difficulty in processing the information they collected. It concluded that the two agencies failed to counter al-Qaida even though they had known for years that Osama bin Laden was determined to mount an attack on American soil. One FBI agent in particular had loudly sounded the tocsin years earlier—a paradoxical, complex figure named John P. O'Neill. In June 1997 in Chicago, in what would become a canned speech, he warned that al-Qaida and allied groups had established a beachhead in America. "Almost all of the groups today, if they chose to, have the ability to strike here in the United States," he said. Two years earlier O'Neill had been appointed head of the Bureau's counterterrorism section in Washington, and he went on to head up the mission in the New York office, considered the nerve center for the entire country. He became the FBI's most committed tracker of bin Laden and his al-Qaida network as they struck around the globe. O'Neill knew his stuff, and he was passionate about it, but there was a question of whether he had the right stuff to be handling counterintelligence.

He never would have made it in MI5, which operates in the dark. As described in *The New Yorker* of January 14, 2002, "O'Neill entered the bureau in the J. Edgar Hoover era, and throughout his career he had something of the old-time G-man about him. He talked tough, in a New Jersey accent that many loved to imitate. He was darkly handsome, with black eyes and slicked-back hair. In a culture that favors discreet anonymity, he cut a memorable figure. He favored fine cigars and Chivas Regal and water with a twist, and carried a nine-millimetre automatic strapped to his ankle. His manner was bluff and dominating, but he was always immaculately, even fussily, dressed." In New York he held court like a celebrity at Elaine's and Bruno's, and due to his relentlessness was dubbed the Count and Prince of Darkness. He was obsessive and compulsive in everything he did, which accounted for a tangled love life. He had such a forceful personality that agents either loved or hated him.

Richard Clarke, the crusty national security advisor, recalled O'Neill's near-manic sense of mission. "John had the same problems with the bureaucracy that I had," Clarke told *The New Yorker*. "Prior to September 11th, a lot of people who were working full time on terrorism thought it was no more than a nuisance. They didn't understand that Al Qaeda was enormously powerful and insidious and that it was not going to stop until it really hurt us. John and some other senior officials knew that. The impatience really grew in us as we dealt with the dolts who didn't understand." Part of the problem was that no one seemed to realize Osama bin Laden's true role. His name had turned up on a list of donors to an Islamic char-

ity that contributed financially to the first World Trade Center bombing, and defendants in the case referred to a "Sheikh Osama" in an
intercepted conversation. Clarke recounted: "They clearly had
money. We'd see CIA reports that referred to 'financier Osama bin
Laden' and we'd ask ourselves, 'Who the hell is he?' The more we
drilled down the more we realized that he was not just a financier—
he was the leader. John said, 'We've got to get this guy. He's building a network. Everything leads back to him.' Gradually, the CIA
came along with us."

In 1994 then-FBI Director Louis Freeh, who had a reputation as
a Mafia-busting street agent while assigned to the New York office,
persuaded President Bill Clinton to issue a directive authorizing
the FBI to investigate crimes against American interests abroad. This
put the National Security Division in the business of criminal investigation, preparing cases for trial in the United States, which
meant it had split responsibilities. O'Neill was playing G-man again,
a role he relished. His first arrest was that of Ramzi Yousef, the brains
behind the 1993 World Trade Center bombing, who had plotted the
aerial bombings of American airliners in Asia. The fugitive was spotted by Pakistani authorities, and O'Neill rushed there to put the
collar on him. In what would be a moment of high irony, O'Neill
mockingly pointed out to his prisoner, as they flew over Manhattan
in a helicopter en route from JFK International Airport to a federal
jail, that the twin towers were still standing. In June 1996, O'Neill
led a team to the scene of the Khobar Towers bombing in Saudi
Arabia that took the lives of nineteen American soldiers. But O'Neill
perceived that the Saudis were impeding the investigation, which
prompted Louis Freeh to intercede. Richard Clarke recounted:
"John told me that, after one of the many trips he and Freeh took to
the Mideast to get better cooperation from the Saudis, they boarded

the Gulfstream to come home and Freeh says, 'Wasn't that a great trip? I think they're really going to help us.' And John says, 'You've got to be kidding. They didn't give us anything. They were just shining sunshine up your ass.' For the next twelve hours, Freeh didn't say another word to him."

The October 2000 bombing in Yemen provided a look at O'Neill as a bull in a china shop. He stormed ashore in the constitutional democracy with a force of three hundred G-men, a support staff and fifty marines toting automatic weapons. He hectored Yemeni authorities to waive their sovereignty by stepping aside so he could take over the investigation. They didn't, and arrested nine suspects on their own. U.S. Ambassador Barbara Bodine was disgusted with O'Neill's ham-fisted approach. "You want a bunch of six-foot-two Irish-Americans to go door to door?" Bodine braced him. "And, excuse me, but how many of your guys speak Arabic?" After he repaired to Washington, she barred him from returning.

Right up to the end of his FBI career, O'Neill warned that America was "due" for attacks by al-Qaida. But for all his frantic investigating of al-Qaida, he never dug up the buried cells in this country, didn't "roll up" the Atta cell. It would have taken someone more reflective, more analytical, more deliberate. He was, in the end, more temperamentally suited to going after organized crime, where he could operate in his gangbuster style.

He finished his FBI career in an ignominious fashion. In the fateful summer of 2001, O'Neill left his briefcase in a Tampa, Florida, hotel conference room while attending an FBI conclave. According to the *New York Times*, the briefcase contained a report detailing every counterintelligence program in New York and describing the manpower assignments for each. When police later recovered the briefcase, only a watch and other personal valuables were missing—the documents were untouched. O'Neill's boss, Barry Mawn, the assistant director in charge of the New York office, waved off the security breach, expressing "complete confidence" in his terrorism expert. But O'Neill had powerful enemies among the hierarchy in Washington who resented his status of living legend. A criminal investigation was begun, and although it was subsequently dropped, the damage to his career was fatal. John O'Neill accepted a position at double his Bureau pay as security chief for the World Trade Center. He was only two weeks into the job when the 9/11 attacks came. He perished along with some three thousand others.

In October 2003 the FBI, bowing to the clamor for architectural change, rolled out its latest model to the accompaniment of much fanfare. "NEW RULES MAKE FBI SPY AGENCY," was one newspaper banner. FBI counterterrorism chief John Pistole, in an interview with Dan Eggen of the *Washington Post*, hailed the new look. "With 9/11 as the catalyst for this, what we've done is fundamentally change the approach we take to every counterterrorism case," Pistole said. "This is a sea change for the FBI." But a closer look revealed that the "sea change" was actually a retrofitting of the pre-9/11 Bureau, bringing in criminal agents to work alongside counterintelligence specialists on the same squads, a mix that had a record of failure. Nothing about improving the quality of the agent corps, nothing about breaking up the congealed mass that is Bureau middle management, nothing about recruiting new agents for their suitability to the complex challenge of counterintelligence work. In fact, the ulterior motive behind breaking down the wall between the criminal and intelligence sides seems to have been the acquisition of expanded search-and-seizure powers. In this the criminal agents are legal pawns, enabling the FBI to conduct many more searches and seizures in secret, as allowed under intelligence laws, rather than being constrained by the rules of traditional criminal warrants. "By eliminating any distinction between criminal and intelligence classifications, it reduces the respect for the ordinary constitutional protections that people have," Joshua Dratel, a New York attorney who has filed legal briefs in opposition to dubious antiterrorism policies, told the *Washington Post* on December 13, 2003, "It will result in a funneling of all cases into an intelligence mode. It's an end run around the Fourth Amendment."

In neglecting meaningful reform of the FBI, indeed, in actively thwarting the creation of a Homeland Intelligence Agency, George W. Bush has rendered America more vulnerable to attack, to another Big One. On September 10, 2003, in an address to FBI employees at the agency's Quantico, Virginia, crime laboratory, the president praised the Bureau as "fully engaged" in the war on terrorism because "the left hand now knows what the right hand is doing." In point of fact, the FBI has not substantially changed from the outfit that flunked its terrorism test on 9/11. The soccer moms of America cannot sleep better at night knowing Bush is their president.

8

THE WAR ON FREEDOM

Within days of the 9/11 attacks, Attorney General John Ashcroft went before the television cameras to argue that the FBI was fatally handicapped in its mission to protect the nation from terrorism by a dearth of wiretapping authority. He complained that the Bureau had no permission to tap the disposable cell phones supposedly now in use by terrorist cells, as if that explained the total intelligence breakdown that allowed the attacks to happen. What he didn't say was that all along the FBI had authority under the Foreign Intelligence Surveillance Act of 1978 (FISA) to tap, bug, and burglarize terrorism or spy suspects. Oversight was provided by a secret court that heard requests for permission in each instance. Located in a sixth-floor bunker of a room in the Justice Department, the court holds sessions every two weeks presided over by a judge from one of seven rotating district courts. In emergencies the FBI can act on its own, subject to subsequent ratification by the court. At one time the FISA requests were approved almost automatically, but in recent years there were some rejections by judges who caught on that Bureau agents were misrepresenting the facts. But there is no reason to believe that the court would use a legal technicality such as "disposable" to deny a request. The language of the law doesn't specifically exclude disposable phones; it refers to phones in general. If the FBI had lost credibility with the court because of its own misconduct, that is another matter.

But the case of Zacarias Moussaoui, which was the FBI's monumental blunder, didn't involve a disposable phone. Moussaoui was the Moroccan ethnic who showed up at a Minneapolis flight school a few weeks before 9/11 wanting to learn how to fly "one of these Big Birds," as he put it in an e-mail to the school—a Boeing 747-400 or Airbus A-300. But he didn't need to know how to take off or land, a sure tip-off he intended to hijack a jumbo aircraft in flight and deliberately crash it. He paid $6,800 of the $8,300 tuition in cash. French intelligence had him on a watch list as connected to Islamic extremists, which fulfilled the FISA requirement that he be linked to a "foreign political faction." The circumstances screamed out for a FISA warrant to electronically monitor him and surreptitiously search his computer's hard drive for evidence of who he was in contact with (after 9/11 provided evidence linking him to the hijackers, the FBI finally downloaded the computer, finding entries concerning airplanes, crop dusting and wind currents). But risk-averse supervisors at Bureau headquarters found the evidence not compelling enough to submit to the FISA court for approval.

The joker in this deck is that the FBI didn't need FISA approval to search Moussaoui's computer. Long on the books was permission to search for evidence incidental to arrest. Moussaoui was taken into custody for having an expired visa in his hotel room, which meant that the room and every object in it, including the computer, could be searched. When I was in the FBI, I used to time an arrest for when a suspect was home, in his car or in his place of business, depending on where I thought the evidence would be. But in its schizophrenia over whether it was working a criminal case or counterintelligence matter, the Bureau didn't search until it was too late.

A comparison between the FBI's unduly cautious approach before 9/11 and that of the CIA is provided by the pro tem National Commission on Terrorism, set up in response to the 1998 bombings of American embassies in East Africa. Headed by L. Paul Bremer, now the U.S. occupation proconsul for Iraq, the commission didn't focus sharply enough on the quality of the FBI and CIA performance, leading to a false confidence in their abilities by issuing generally complimentary reviews. But an insight into the CIA's proclivity to ignore fine points was given by Agency spokesman Bill Harlow when the commission's final report was released in June 2000. Asked if the CIA felt hamstrung by a recommendation that its agents in place overseas have clean human rights records, Harlow replied, "The bottom line is, CIA headquarters has never turned down a request to use someone — even someone with a human rights abuse — if we thought that person could be valuable to our counter-terrorism program." The commission was critical of the FBI, saying that it was too risk-averse to be effective.

If the FBI had followed the commission's advice and become more aggressive in its campaign against terrorism, using the tools it had, 9/11 might have been prevented. So it was disingenuous of Ashcroft to represent that the FBI had not been given a free hand, that it was in a legal straitjacket. If the Bureau itself had felt that it needed specific authority to tap disposable phones, that it was a vital necessity, it could have gone to Congress with a request to amend FISA. The FBI has never been bashful about seeking what it wants, and Congress never turned down a reasonable request. In

1999 the ambitious director Louis Freeh, who had made his mark as a field agent by going after the Mafia in New York, sought and got extraterritorial jurisdiction for his agency to investigate abroad and bring back terrorist suspects for prosecution, bypassing the courts of the country where the crime occurred. The legislation was justified, Freeh said, by the 1998 bombing of the U.S. Embassy in Kenya, in which the al-Qaida suspects were identified by the investigative efforts of the Kenyan police. What this illustrates once again is the FBI's concentration on its law enforcement function, solving and prosecuting crimes after they happen, to the detriment of its counterintelligence responsibilities, ferreting out terrorist cells before they can commit the crimes.

Ashcroft's bleat about disposable phones was just the opening shot in his drive to exponentially expand the powers of the FBI. He did it for the most part through a loosely drafted, sweeping piece of legislation called the USA Patriot Act, which defined a terrorist as anyone the FBI wanted to so categorize. Members of Congress were stampeded into passing the act under pain of being labeled unpatriotic or worse. But it has unfortunate historical precedents that demonstrate that draconian measures such as mass detentions are unnecessary—they simply are a cover for the proven incompetence of the intelligence agencies—totalitarian methods for keeping the masses in line by intimidation. It is déjà vu all over again.

In the wake of the 9/11 attacks, Ashcroft ordered a roundup of more than a thousand people profiled as being possible suspects, mostly through their Middle Eastern ethos, and detained them indefinitely without charges. Many were held incommunicado, and not even their families were notified they were in custody. Interrogated by the FBI, the noncitizens among them were threatened with deportation to a foreign country that employed torture if they didn't confess. Ashcroft tried to silence critics with the menacing retort, "Your tactics only aid terrorists. They give ammunition to America's enemies." It was an eerie echo of J. Edgar Hoover's Red Raids in 1919–1920 following a spate of bombings gratuitously attributed to anarchists. Hoover, then a young and zealous Justice Department aide, compiled 450,000 index cards of putative radicals, profiling them through a mix of rumor, gossip and fact. He then orchestrated dragnet detentions based on the cards. But no one was ever criminally charged in the bombings. Like Hoover, Ashcroft disdained open court, where traditional American standards of proof are required. In the first judicial test of his policy, however, he was stingingly rebuked. In August 2002, a federal appeals court in Cincinnati unanimously ruled that he had acted unlawfully by holding hundreds of deportation hearings in secret, based solely on the government's assertion of links to terrorism. "Democracies die behind closed doors," wrote Judge Damon Keith.

Ashcroft's groping methods of trying to disrupt terrorists have instead disrupted people's lives. He ordered the FBI to interrogate en masse men of Middle Eastern origin without a shred of evidence that they were somehow involved in terrorism. The numbers on the interrogation lists were so daunting that the Bureau had to ask police departments for help. But some chiefs of police, among them those of San Francisco and Portland, Oregon, refused to cooperate with a fishing expedition. The chief in Milpitas, a Silicon Valley city with a large Afghan population, lent his cops to the interrogations only to guard the men from FBI intimidation.

Ashcroft also authorized a program called Operation TIPS that would have set up a nationwide network of utility workers, postal carriers, meter readers, telephone repairmen and others given routine access to private property to report anything "suspicious" they see or hear on a confidential hot line. Operation TIPS harkens back to the Red-under-every-bed hysteria whipped up by Hoover during the McCarthy era to encourage neighbors to spy on neighbors. The result was a flood of accusations by people with personal grudges or extreme right-wing views, which sowed the seeds of suspicion across the land. What the public didn't know in those Cold War days was that the Communist Party USA was a paper tiger fed survival rations by Hoover to maintain the illusion that only he stood between democracy and a communist takeover. By 1960 CPUSA membership had dwindled to 6,000, some 1,600 of whom were FBI informants. The informants' dues, paid with Bureau money, were the CPUSA's largest source of funding. Penetration reached to the highest echelon. In the early 1950s Morris and Jack Childs, functionaries who felt slighted, became FBI informants in Chicago and New York. The brothers rose in the CPUSA to a status where Morris, handled by Bureau agents Carl Freyman and Walter Boyle, traveled to Moscow and Beijing as the second-ranking CPUSA official, meeting with Nikita Khrushchev and Mao Tse-tung. From the Kremlin, Morris would bring back a cash transfusion to be pumped into party coffers by Jack, who was handled by agent Alexander Burlinson. Morris and Jack reported to the CPUSA's top boss, General Secretary Gus Hall, whose name became synonymous with the CPUSA during this period. What I learned only recently, from an FBI source, was that Gus Hall himself was a paid Bureau informant, handled by agent Boyle.

So the FBI has always relied to a great extent on informants, needing no statutory authority. With no statutory authority, it makes up its own rules, which can be hazardous to civil rights. The problem with informants is that they are perforce part of the milieu under investigation, be it the CPUSA, the Mafia or al-Qaida, and are paid commensurate with their productivity, making them prone to exaggerate or even fabricate to gain a handsome payday. And the system can breed corruption, as the recent conviction of agent John Connolly of the Boston office illustrates. In the 1960s Connolly developed an informant named James "Whitey" Bulger of the Winter Hill Gang, which was in a turf war with the local Mafia. Connolly shielded Bulger and his gang while they committed, the local authorities charged, nineteen murders and framed innocent men, putting two of them on death row. Lawsuits have been filed by the families of the victims in an amount exceeding $300 million, and Ashcroft resisted turning over more documents relevant to the cases. Ones previously produced, however, are indicting. On June 4, 1965, J. Edgar Hoover dunned the Boston field division on what was being done to develop a Bulger lieutenant, Vincent Flemmi, as an informant. Five days later, the agent in charge at Boston replied that Flemmi was known to have killed eight men, and, "from all indications, he is going to continue to commit murder." Nevertheless, the agent said, "the informant's potential outweighs the risk involved." Hoover did not order that a serial murderer be disqualified as a Bureau informant. In 1968, after the framed men were convicted, he sent a letter of commendation to the Boston agents.

The FBI's cavalier attitude toward the Constitution and the Bill of Rights is deeply rooted in the Hoover regime. On the otherwise insignificant date of February 5, 1951, when I was sworn in as a special agent of the Federal Bureau of Investigation, I vowed to uphold the Constitution of the United States. That was the last I heard about the Constitution — or the Bill of Rights for that matter — during a ten-year career in which I worked criminal and counterintelligence cases as well as served as a supervisor and inspector. Those documents at the heart of our democracy were never mentioned.

Not even when I was trained in the Bureau's secret Sound School in the black arts of wiretapping, bugging and breaking in. The only caveat was that break-ins were illegal, the message being "Don't get caught." "Possession of burglary tools can get you seven years," warned George Berley, the Bureau's crack safecracker who taught me all I knew and provided me with the burglary tools, as a parting shot as he turned me loose to ply my new trade.

As a member of the select circle of Sound Men, I ignored the Constitution by participating in the lawless law enforcement. Practically all of it fell under the catchphrase of "national security." The "black bag jobs," as the break-ins were called, were pulled off to photograph documents or plant listening devices, and they were rampant. One of my colleagues in the New York office was a full-time burglar, earning regular cash "meritorious" awards from the chief. To avoid embarrassing the Bureau, we were instructed not to carry anything that might link us to the mother church—no gun, no badge, no insurance card. The local police were asked to overlook any report of a burglary in progress in the target neighborhood. If we were caught, our superiors would in time arrange to quietly effect our release. All records of the capers were filed in a sensitive Do Not File file, to be destroyed after three months.

Much of the information gained by illicit means was used to fan the hysteria over communism generated by Hoover, who was firing off abstracts to Joe McCarthy to aid in his witch hunt. Lives, reputations and careers were destroyed. It was the onset of COINTELPRO, a program of dirty tricks in which, for example, agents anonymously phoned employers to hint that they were employing a communist, a term used as loosely then as terrorist is today, with the aim of inducing a pink slip. One of the most infamous COINTELPRO tricks was the anonymous letter mailed to Dr. Martin Luther King Jr., accusing him of sexual orgies and suggesting he commit suicide; the letter was addressed so that his wife would see it first. One of the sickest was the destruction of actress Jean Seberg, who played the title role in *Joan of Arc*, because she supported the Black Panthers. In 1969 a wiretap revealed that Seberg was pregnant. The FBI anonymously leaked the news, inferring that a Black Panthers member was the father. Following a publicity cloudburst, the emotionally fragile Seberg took an overdose of sleeping pills, and the baby survived only two days after being born. She became obsessed over the baby's death, the more so when, several years later, she learned of the FBI's dirty trick. In 1979 Seberg committed suicide. Her former husband, French novelist Romain Gary, gave the epitaph, "Jean Seberg was destroyed by the FBI."

I was opposed in principle to COINTELPRO, the more so because information obtained through illicit bugs and break-ins was being exploited. So in 1966, after decamping from the FBI, I wrote an exposé called "I Was a Burglar, Bugger, Wiretapper and Spy for the FBI," published in *Ramparts* magazine. National columnist Drew Pearson picked up on it, and Nevada Governor Grant Sawyer asked me to do television spots for his reelection campaign in which FBI bugging of casinos was an issue. Although I didn't learn it until years later, Hoover ordered a halt to black bag jobs because they were now too risky. Ironically, Congress, still intimidated by Hoover's possession of personal files on just about every member, remained supine. The matter was a time bomb that wouldn't go off until 1972, when the Watergate burglars were caught in the act. Richard Nixon tried to justify the crime by contending that Democratic Presidents John Kennedy and Lyndon Johnson had authorized the FBI to conduct break-ins, which was untrue. When the Associated Press called me from Washington, I let the cat out of the bag by disclosing that agents, myself included, had pulled off black bag jobs under President Dwight Eisenhower and his vice president, Richard Nixon. The wire story was headed, "Ex-Agent Bares Break-ins Under Ike." And I talked about "suicide taps"—ones bootlegged by overly zealous agents that were not approved by any internal authority. The USA Patriot Act is an invitation to such vigilantes.

Since Hoover had died weeks before the Watergate scandal erupted, Congress mustered the courage to investigate the wrongdoings of the intelligence agencies—the CIA was on the griddle for its attempts to assassinate foreign leaders—and bring them under control. I was called to testify before Representative Robert Kastenmeier's House Subcommittee on Administrative Practice and Procedure, two of whose members were Father Joseph Drinnen, the liberal Jesuit, and William Cohen, future secretary of defense under Bill Clinton. But when the Reagan administration took over, the intelligence agencies were unleashed again. In the war on terrorism, there was no need for anything like the USA Patriot Act. The FBI was inhibited only by its garbled sense of mission and its inherent incompetence.

An example of the latter can be found in the Bureau's profiling of suspects. Criticism has been leveled against the practice on grounds that it is politically incorrect—yes, racist—to profile every male of Middle East extraction as a potential terrorist. My complaint would be that, despite the movie *Silence of the Lambs* in which an ambitious FBI agent uses psychiatric profiling to capture a serial killer, profiling is a quirky art that can cause too much reliance on a focus that is totally wrong, drawing attention away from the real criminal. Richard Reid, who tried to set off a shoe bomb on an American Airlines jet from Paris to Miami but was overpowered by a flight attendant and passengers, is white English. More and more

suicide bombers are women. And the Unabomber, a domestic ter-
rorist, wasn't an electrician. In an op-ed piece in the *San Francisco
Chronicle* on June 30, 2002, titled "Wanted—A New Breed of FBI
Agent," I wrote:

> Beginning in 1978, a terrorist code-named the Unabomber
> mailed off a total of 15 package bombs that exploded, one on an
> airliner in flight, killing two people and maiming a number of
> others. The FBI drew a profile of the Unabomber as a blue-
> collar type, possibly an electrician or plumber. I disagreed. He
> was an academic associated in the past with a San Francisco area
> university. I conveyed this to the FBI. Two years later, in 1996,
> the Unabomber's brother turned him in (otherwise, the Bureau
> might still be looking for him). He turned out to be Ted
> Kaczynski, a former mathematics instructor at the University of
> California at Berkeley.

The degree of contempt John Ashcroft holds for an open society
can be measured by his sneak attack on the Freedom of Information Act (FOIA), which empowered citizens to gain access to government files with certain restrictions. FOIA has been a formidable
tool for holding federal authorities accountable for their actions. As
the *San Francisco Chronicle* put it on October 12, 2002, "Most Americans had no idea that one of their most precious freedoms disappeared on October 12. Yet it happened. In a memo that slipped
beneath the political radar, Ashcroft vigorously urged federal agencies [including the FBI and CIA] to resist most Freedom of Information Act requests made by American citizens. Passed in 1974 in
the wake of the Watergate scandal, the Freedom of Information Act
has been hailed as one of our greatest democratic reforms." What
Ashcroft was telling the agencies was, you stonewall the requests,
and I'll use the full power of the Justice Department to back you up.
In short, he was suborning breaking the law. Paradoxically, he defended
himself against comparison with J. Edgar Hoover by pointing out

that Hoover acted illegally. It would seem that the attorney general was saying that he had legal cover to break one law by invoking another: the USA Patriot Act. If so, it is testimony as to how ambiguously the USA Patriot Act was crafted. The bulk of Freedom of Information Act requests have nothing to do with terrorism, yet Ashcroft is shutting down the entire process.

That may be because he doesn't want evidence of the extent of government spying on citizens, and the illicit activities that go with it, to become public knowledge. How are the "no fly" lists used to bar individuals on it from air travel compiled? It's a secret. Of what possible use to the war on terrorism is the government's edict to libraries to turn over records of who checked out what books? It's a secret. (Some librarians found this so Big Brother they shredded the records rather than turn them over to the FBI.) The expansion of FBI powers to demand records from the business spectrum—casinos, car dealerships, banks, to name three—without seeking court approval? It's a secret. Not a secret is Ashcroft's decision to allow the FBI to return to the political spying of the Hoover era. It came to light through a confidential Bureau memorandum circulated to police departments in October 2003 in advance of massive anti–Iraq war demonstrations in Washington and San Francisco, a copy of which was obtained by Eric Lichtblau of the *New York Times*. According to Lichtblau in his story of November 22, 2003, "The Federal Bureau of Investigation has collected extensive information on the tactics, training and organization of antiwar demonstrators and has advised local law enforcement officials to report any suspicious activity at protests to its counterterrorism squads." The memorandum, the story said, "detailed how protesters have sometimes used 'training camps' to rehearse for demonstrations, the Internet to raise money and gas masks to defend against tear gas.

The memorandum analyzed lawful activities like recruiting demonstrators, as well as illegal activities like using fake documentation to get into a secured site." The allusion to "training camps" is inflammatory, likening as it does the war protest leaders' storefronts to bin Laden's Afghan training camps. According to Lichtblau, "FBI officials said in interviews that the intelligence-gathering effort was aimed at anarchists and 'extremist elements' plotting violence, not at monitoring the political speech of law-abiding protesters." What the Bureau chose to ignore was that the protesters' ranks included unprecedented numbers of plain moms and pops, the elderly, veterans of past wars, techies and businesspeople; a protest leader in San Francisco was an executive of the Pacific Stock Exchange. There was no violence.

In his piece, Lichtblau quoted Anthony Romero, executive director of the American Civil Liberties Union: "The line between terrorism and legitimate civil disobedience is blurred, and I have a serious concern about whether we're going back to the days of Hoover." Since it is difficult to see what spying on demonstrators has to do with rooting out al-Qaida cells, it is reasonable to conclude that Ashcroft has more blanketing surveillance of dissidents in mind. Warrantless bugging, tapping and black bag jobs, along with COINTELPRO operations and a return to Hoover's intimidating dossier system, are the next step in the creation of a national security state.

The ultimate extension of the national security state — abandonment of the Constitution in favor of a military takeover — is a live possibility. This spooky appraisal came from no less an authority than General Tommy Franks, who led the invasion of Iraq, in an interview after retiring in the December 2003 issue of *Cigar Aficionado* magazine. Discussing the hypothetical dangers facing the

United States in the wake of 9/11, Franks said that "the worst thing that could happen" is if terrorists acquire and then use a biological, chemical or nuclear weapon that inflicts heavy casualties. In that event, Franks stated, "the Western world, the free world, loses what it cherishes most, and that is freedom and liberty we've seen for a couple of hundred years in this grand experiment that we call democracy." Franks then offered "in a practical sense" what he thought would happen in the aftermath of such an attack. "It means the potential of a weapon of mass destruction and a terrorist, massive, casualty-producing event somewhere in the Western world—it may be in the United States of America—that causes our population to question our own Constitution and to begin to militarize our country in order to avoid a repeat of another [sic] mass, casualty-producing event. Which in fact then begins to unravel the fabric of our Constitution. Two steps, very, very important." The supreme irony here is that the invasion of Iraq led by Franks had nothing to do with the war on terrorism; it was an oil-grab diversion in the guise of liberty. In fact, the diversion compromised the search to find Osama bin Laden and crush al-Qaida by pulling out the paramilitary and intelligence resources directed at them in Afghanistan and redeploying them to Iraq. Even the spy satellites were yanked and retrained on Saddam Hussein. As a result, bin Laden and al-Qaida were given a window of opportunity to regroup and recruit new blood. They did so with a vengeance, as the skein of deadly bombings around the Middle East and the globe demonstrated. Thanks to the window, there is more than ever the possibility of another Big One hitting America. And to be sure, it won't be Saddam who sets it off.

In a ringing 2003 address before the American Constitution Society, former Vice President Al Gore lashed out at the Bush administration's sophistry in pursuing the war on terrorism in an Orwellian fashion. "I want to challenge the Bush administration's implicit assumption that we have to give up many of our traditional freedoms in order to be safe from terrorists," he said. "In fact, in my opinion, it makes no more sense to launch an assault on our civil liberties as the best way to get at terrorists than it did to launch an invasion of Iraq as the best way to get at Osama bin Laden." Gore went on, "Rather than defending our freedoms, this administration has sought to abandon them. Rather than accepting our traditions of openness and accountability, this administration has opted to rule by secrecy and unquestioned authority. Its assaults on our core democratic principles have left us less free and less secure." In his peroration, Gore declared what is at stake: "Will we continue to live as a people under the rule of law as embodied in our Constitution? Or will we fail future generations, by leaving them a Constitution far diminished from the charter of liberty we have inherited from our forebears? Our choice is clear."

The dragnet approach to the menace of terrorism is implicitly an admission by the Bush administration that it is incapable of dealing with it in a focused way. It is also unproductive. In a December 8, 2003, article, "Terror Arrests Impressive, Prosecutions Not, Says Study," United Press International reporter Shaun Waterman led in, "Of the thousands of people referred by the FBI and other federal investigators to prosecutors in connection with terrorism since the September 11 attacks, only a handful have been convicted and sentenced to long prison terms, according to a new analysis of Justice Department figures." The analysis was carried out by statisticians and longtime law enforcement observers at the Transactional Records Access Clearinghouse (TRAC) based at Syracuse University. It found that in the two years after the attacks, about 6,400 people were referred to prosecutors in connection with terrorism or terrorist offenses. But of the 2,681 cases that had been wrapped up, only 879 resulted in a criminal conviction, and less than half of those—373—were sent to prison. Only five received sentences of twenty years or more, *which was fewer than in the two years before 9/11 under the Clinton administration* [italics added]. Most of the convictions were on peripheral technical charges such as immigration violations. None were for conspiring to commit a terrorist act, which the FBI defines as "the unlawful use of force or violence committed by a group or individual, who has some connection to a foreign power or whose activities transcend national boundaries, against persons or property to intimidate or coerce a government, the civilian population, or any segment thereof, in furtherance of political or social objectives."

Not even the touted convictions of the "Lackawanna Six" fit that bill. The defendants, residents of the Buffalo suburb, were devout Muslims who made a pilgrimage to an Islamic studies school in Pakistan several months before 9/11 and while there made a side trip across the border to an al-Qaida camp in Afghanistan. Back in Lackawanna they talked openly about it, and a tipster notified the FBI. Agents clamped a surveillance on them but detected no overt acts in furtherance of a conspiracy. So they were prosecuted for "supporting" terrorism—the side trip to the camp. It was hardly a roll-up of an active terrorist cell, but the "Lackawanna Six" were sentenced to more than five years.

The American Civil Liberties Union commented that the TRAC analysis "punctures the hype that the Justice Department and government have used to justify the Patriot Act and other measures they say are needed to fight terrorism." FBI spokesman Jim Parsell countered that the analysis was out of context—there was an administrative requirement for every case investigated to be referred to prosecutors so it could be closed, even when there was no prospect of a successful prosecution. But there was a story behind that story. As Al Gore put it, referring to the treatment of immigrants, "Let's be clear about what happened: this was little more than a cheap and cruel political stunt by John Ashcroft. More than 99 percent of the mostly Arab-background men who were rounded up had merely overstayed their visas or committed some other minor offense as they tried to pursue the American dream, just like most immigrants. But they were used as extras in the administration's effort to give the impression that they had caught a large number of bad guys. And many of them were treated horribly and abusively."

As an example, Gore cited a column by Anthony Lewis of the *New York Times*:

> Anser Mehmood, a Pakistani who had overstayed his visa, was arrested in New York on October 3, 2001. The next day he was briefly questioned by FBI agents, who said they had no further interest in him. Then he was shackled in handcuffs, leg irons, and a belly chain and taken to the Metropolitan Detention Center in Brooklyn. Guards there put two more sets of handcuffs on him and another set of leg irons. One threw Mehmood against a wall. The guards forced him to run down a long ramp, the irons cutting into his wrists and ankles. The physical abuse was mixed with verbal taunts.
>
> After two weeks Mehmood was allowed to make a telephone call to his wife. She was not at home and Mehmood was told that he would have to wait six weeks to try again. He first saw her, on a visit, three months after his arrest. All that time he was kept in a windowless cell, in solitary confinement, with two overhead fluorescent lights on all the time. In the end he was charged with using an invalid Social Security card. He was deported in May 2002, nearly eight months after his arrest.

Throwing Ashcroft's religiosity back at him, Lewis quoted the teaching from Jesus, "Whatsoever you do unto the least of my brethren, you do unto me." From a practical standpoint as well, this kind of treatment was self-defeating. It created tremendous resentment in immigrant communities, lessening the chance of cooperation in the war on terrorism.

The judicial branch is at least trying to limit the damage to American values the Bush administration has inflicted. On December 18, 2003, appellate courts in New York and San Francisco ruled that the administration overstepped its bounds in detaining suspects, issuing decisions that favored key civil liberties over government power. The New York judges ruled in the case of Jose Padilla, the Chicagoan who was arrested by the FBI in May 2002 as he stepped off a plane in the Windy City. An al-Qaida operative captured in Pakistan had tattled on Padilla that he intended to detonate a "dirty bomb" in the United States, but the FBI didn't find any evidence to corroborate the story. Without any reliable evidence to prosecute Padilla in a federal court, President Bush declared him an "enemy combatant" and he was lodged incommunicado in a Navy brig. The court held that Bush does not have the power to declare a U.S. citizen an "enemy combatant" to be detained indefinitely, and ordered him released from the brig for possible prosecution in federal court with full rights as a citizen. The denouement was actually the government's fault to begin with. What the FBI should have done when Padilla stepped off the plane was place him under surveillance to see whether he would make any move toward building a dirty bomb. But agents were afraid of losing the tail and nabbed him on the spot.

The San Francisco decision concerned the "enemy combatant" designation as well, this time over the Guantanamo 650, foreign citizens of Afghanistan, Iraq, Pakistan, Canada, Britain and other countries who were scooped up overseas and deposited in the U.S. detention camp at the Guantanamo naval base in Cuba. They were being held incommunicado without legal counsel and subjected to exhaustive interrogation, but no charges were filed so that the evidence against them, if any, was recondite. Their release would come at the end of the war on terrorism, the government decreed, at the same time saying there was no end in sight. It was straight out of Kafka. "We simply cannot accept the government's position," wrote Judge Stephen Reinhardt, "that the executive branch possesses the unchecked authority to imprison indefinitely any persons, foreign citizens included, on territory under the sole jurisdiction and control of the United States, without permitting such prisoners recourse of any kind to any judicial forum, or even access to counsel, regardless of the length or manner of their confinement."

That eloquence was lost on the Bush administration, which tried to overthrow both decisions.

Although professing to be a champion of free speech, Bush's actions belie his words. When he travels around the United States, the Secret Service visits the location ahead of time and instructs the local police to set up "free speech zones" or "protest zones" where people opposed to Bush are quarantined. This keeps protesters out of the president's sight and outside the view of the media covering the event.

James Bovard, writing in the *American Conservative* December 15, 2003, tells of one such event:

> When Bush went to the Pittsburgh area on Labor Day 2002, 65-year-old retired steel worker Bill Neel was there to greet him with a sign proclaiming "The Bush Family Must Surely Love the Poor, They Made So Many of Us." The local police, at the Secret Service's behest, set up a "designated free speech zone" on a baseball field surrounded by a chain-link fence a third of a

mile from the location of Bush's speech. The police cleared the path of the motorcade of all critical signs, but folks with pro-Bush signs were permitted to line the president's path. Neel refused to go to the designated area and was arrested for disorderly conduct; the police also confiscated his sign. Neel later commented, "As far as I'm concerned, the whole country is a free-speech zone. If the Bush administration has its way, anyone who criticizes them will be out of sight and out of mind."

Pennsylvania District Judge Shirley Rowe Trkula had the last word. Tossing the disorderly conduct charge, she declaimed, "I believe this is America. Whatever happened to 'I don't agree with you, but I'll defend to the death your right to say it?'"

In addition to constitutional rights, Bush is a gross violator of human rights by dint of signing a secret presidential "finding" permitting torture by proxy. Christopher H. Pyle, a teacher of civil liberties at Mount Holyoke College, cited the case of Maher Arar, a Syrian-born Canadian citizen, in the *San Francisco Chronicle* on January 4, 2004. On September 26, 2002, Arar was about to change planes at Kennedy International Airport on his way home to Canada after visiting his wife's family in Tunisia when U.S. immigration officers pulled him aside for interrogation. As Pyle put it, "He was not a terrorist. He had no terrorist connections, but his name was on the watch list, so he was detained for questioning. Not ordinary, polite questioning, but abusive, insulting, degrading questioning by the immigration service, the FBI and the New York City police department. He asked for a lawyer and was told he could not have one. He asked to call his family, but phone calls were not permitted. Instead, he was clapped into shackles and, for several days, made to 'disappear.' His family was frantic."

Arar resolutely denied any connection to terrorists, and had lived a blameless life in Canada for sixteen years. But the computer had spewed out links so tenuous as to be laughable: The Syrian government thought that a cousin of Arar's mother had been, nine years earlier, long after Arar left for Canada, a member of the Muslim Brotherhood, and the Royal Canadian Mounted Police reported that the lease on Arar's apartment had been witnessed by a Syrian-born Canadian who was believed to know an Egyptian Canadian whose brother was said to be mentioned in an al-Qaida document. If there was anything to this the RCMP, being a competent investigative agency, would have checked it out long ago. But the FBI agents wanted Arar grilled by someone whose methods were more primitive. Pyle recounted what happened next:

> So, they put Arar on a private plane and flew him to Washington, D.C. There, a new team, presumably from the CIA, took over and delivered him, by way of Jordan, to Syrian interrogators. . . . The Syrians locked Arar in an underground cell the size of a grave: 3 feet wide, 6 feet long, 7 feet high. Then they questioned him, under torture, repeatedly, for ten months. Finally, when it was obvious that their prisoner had no terrorist ties, they let him go, 40 pounds lighter, with a pronounced limp and chronic nightmares.

The Arar case is not an exception — torture by proxy is a program called "extraordinary rendition" institutionalized by George Bush with one stroke of the pen. As one intelligence officer explained to Pyle, "We don't kick the shit out of them. We send them to other countries so they can kick the shit out of them." But Pyle wryly notes, "Where the president gets the authority to have anyone tortured has never been explained."

In fact, George W. Bush has appropriated total authority for himself. "I'm the commander — see, I don't need to explain — I do not need to explain why I say things," he is quoted by Bob Woodward in *Bush at War*. "That's the interesting thing about being the president. Maybe somebody needs to explain to me why they say something, but I don't feel like I owe anybody an explanation." He sees himself as above accountability, the true mark of an authoritarian. He and John Ashcroft are in effect telling Benjamin Franklin to go fly a kite when he said, "They that can give up essential liberty to gain a little temporary safety deserve neither liberty nor safety."

Bush and Ashcroft have created a national security state that J. Edgar Hoover could only envy. The pity of it is that the crackdown on civil freedoms has not advanced the cause of safety one whit. In his speech on freedom and security, Al Gore described the Bush administration's assault on civil liberties as un-American, charged that the Bush-Ashcroft attack on the Constitution is actually a smoke screen that obscures their fundamental failure to meaningfully protect our national security, and pointed out that their efforts have weakened rather than strengthened America.

There are those who scoff at Americans concerned about the shutdown of freedom as "handwringers." Let the scoffers be aware that sitting on Ashcroft's desk is a draft of USA Patriot Act II that would, among a host of draconian measures, empower the government to strip Americans of their citizenship if they participate in the *lawful* activities of any group the attorney general designates as terrorist. And an American merely suspected of being part of a terrorist conspiracy could be held by investigators without anyone being notified—in other words, simply disappear. Not even Hoover tried to go that far with the Communist Party, and the chilling part is that the definition of "terrorist" is wide open to the fertile imagination of John Ashcroft.

As Pastor Niemoller expressed it in his Holocaust text, "First they came for the Communists, but I was not a Communist—so I said nothing. Then they came for the Social Democrats, but I was not a

Social Democrat—so I did nothing. And then they came for the Jews, but I was not a Jew—so I did little. And then they came for me, and there was no one left who could stand up for me."

Read it and shudder.

9

'SCREWED UP"

General Anthony C. Zinni is a decorated Vietnam veteran—he was hit by three rounds from an enemy AK-47 assault rifle near Da Nang—a four-star Marine Corps general, and former Central Command Chief in Charge of all U.S. forces in the Persian Gulf Region. In this capacity he oversaw enforcement of the two "no-fly" zones in Iraq and in 1998 conducted four days of punishing air strikes against Saddam Hussein's defense installations code-named Operation Desert Fox. In 2001 President Bush named him Special Envoy to the Middle East at the insistence of his old friend and comrade, Colin Powell. He did consulting work on Iraq for the CIA right up to the beginning of the March 2003 invasion.

And what does he think about that invasion? In an interview by reporter Thomas E. Ricks of the *Washington Post* published December 23, 2003, Zinni bluntly opined that the Bush administration "screwed up" by going to war, going so far as to suggest that Bush as an apprentice president had been "captured" by the neocon ideologues he had appointed to key positions.

Zinni had his first brush with the neocons in 1998 when Paul Wolfowitz took offense to his position on Iraq. The general had long worried that there were worse outcomes possible in Iraq than having Saddam in power—such as taking him out in such a way that Iraq would become a new haven for terrorism in the Middle East. "I think a weakened, fragmented, chaotic Iraq, which could happen if it isn't done carefully, is more dangerous in the long run than a contained Saddam is now," he told reporters in 1998. "I don't think these questions have been thought through." Wolfowitz, then an academic at the University of Chicago, the alma mater of the neocon movement, attacked him in print. As we have seen, that movement was organized a year earlier into the Project for the New American Century, a think tank funded by the defense industry, oil and gas behemoths, and conservative foundations such as the American Enterprise Institute. As early as 1992, Dick Cheney, fresh from his job as the senior George Bush's secretary of defense during Gulf War I, had drawn a blueprint for a radical foreign policy change that rejected traditional values of international cooperation in favor of unilateral action based on American supremacy in culture, economic strength and military might, thus undermining its moral authority. A might-makes-right theory that would force-feed target countries democracy, Halliburton style. In addition to Cheney and Wolfowitz, the superhawks of the Project for the New American Century number Secretary of Defense Donald Rumsfeld, Wolfowitz's boss, and the so-called "Prince of Darkness," Richard Perle, a luminary of the influential Defense Policy Board that advises the Pentagon.

Despite his earlier dustup with Wolfowitz, General Zinni didn't realize that the neocons, after marking time during the Clinton administration, intended to launch a preemptive first strike against

Iraq as one of their first orders of business after taking power under George W. Bush. The moment of truth came in August 2002 at the national convention of the Veterans of Foreign Wars in Nashville at the Opryland Hotel. He was there to receive the VFW's Dwight D. Eisenhower Distinguished Service Award in recognition of his thirty-five years in the Marine Corps. Dick Cheney, who once said he had "other priorities" than soldiering in the Vietnam War, was there as well, delivering a foreign policy speech. As he sat on the stage behind the vice president, Zinni became increasingly puzzled. He had endorsed Bush and Cheney in 2000, just after he had retired as Chief of the Central Command, thinking they were moderately conservative Republicans. Now he was hearing Cheney make a case for a preemptive invasion of Iraq. "Simply stated, there is no doubt that Saddam Hussein now has weapons of mass destruction," Cheney said. "There is no doubt that he is amassing them to use against our friends, against our allies, and against us." The danger was clear and present. "Time is not on our side," Cheney contended. "The risks of inaction are far greater than the risks of action." Zinni was bewildered. As chief of the Central Command, he had been immersed in intelligence about Iraq, and was familiar with intelligence analysts' doubts that Saddam had programs to acquire WMD. "In my time at CentCom, I watched the intelligence," Zinni said. "And never—not once—did it say, 'He has WMD.'"

Zinni approved of the Afghanistan campaign in the wake of the 9/11 attacks, since it was targeted on the perpetrators, Osama bin Laden and his al-Qaida, and the Taliban who were harboring them. But he saw no legitimate reason to knock off Saddam Hussein. "He was contained," Zinni told reporter Ricks. "It was a pain in the ass, but he was contained. He had a deteriorated military. He wasn't a threat to the region." Zinni was called to testify before a Senate panel just six weeks before the invasion. As he awaited his turn, he listened to Pentagon and State Department officials talk vaguely about the "uncertainties" of a postwar Iraq. "I was listening to the panel, and I realized, 'These guys don't have a clue,'" he recalled. The more he heard Wolfowitz and other administration officials talk about Iraq, the more Zinni became persuaded that interventionist "neoconservative" ideologues were plunging the nation into a war in a part of the world they didn't understand. "The more I saw, the more I thought that this was the product of the neocons who didn't understand the region and were going to create havoc there," he said. "These were dilettantes from Washington think tanks who never had an idea that worked on the ground." And the more he dwelled on it, the more he foresaw that American soldiers would end up paying for the mistakes of Beltway policy-makers. "I don't know where the neocons came from—that wasn't the platform they ran on," Zinni stated, as if it was a neocon sleeper cell. "Somehow the neocons captured the president. They captured the vice president."

As reported in the first chapter, Wolfowitz used the lure of oil to seduce Bush into warlike thoughts on Iraq. He told the occupant of the Oval Office that the country's second largest city, Basra, lies "within 60 kilometers of the Kuwaiti border and within 60 percent of Iraq's total oil production." Having pushed through a "regime change" in Baghdad, which had been on their minds for four years, the neocons needed a pretext noir. Wolfowitz admitted that in the discussions WMD were never the most compelling reason proposed. One justification put forth was that the elimination of Saddam would enable the evacuation of American troops securing Saudi Arabia, something the Saudis wanted because Osama bin Laden was ranting on about the presence of "infidel" warriors on the holy soil of

Mecca. Apparently not seriously considered was Saddam's atrocious record on human rights that, ironically, would become the ex post facto rationalization for the invasion; there were scores of other brutal dictatorships around the world. So it was not high moral purpose but practicality that ruled. "For bureaucratic reasons we settled on one issue, weapons of mass destruction," Wolfowitz recounted, "because it was the one reason everyone could agree on."

Having put the WMD cart before the horse, the neocons set out to "prove" the threat. As Zinni pointed out, the CIA was no help—the agency had no convincing evidence of an Iraqi WMD capability. As far as it knew, Saddam had ordered the suspension of WMD development programs after sanctions were imposed following Gulf War I. This was confirmed by Iraqi scientists interviewed before and after the invasion. A top rocket scientist, Modher Sadeq-Saba Tamini, told the *Washington Post* that he had hidden his designs for nine-ton missiles from U.N. inspectors, but that the weapons themselves did not exist. Other scientists who had been involved with Iraq's WMD programs uniformly testified that after Gulf War I they had to look for another line of work. Yet in the wake of 9/11 Dick Cheney made multiple visits to CIA headquarters, trying to cajole its professional analysts to alter their reports. When the analysts refused to turn creative, Wolfowitz turned the assignment over to the Office of Special Plans, which he had created at the Pentagon for just such an eventuality. Manned by neocon policy wonks, the shop was nothing more than a propaganda mill. It interviewed its stable of Iraqi defectors who had a vested interest in the overthrow of Saddam and were more than willing to repeat rumors about big, bad WMD.

So what George Bush and Colin Powell presented to the world as evidence of Iraqi WMD was largely black propaganda created by the Office of Special Plans. Powell at least was so incensed at the flimsiness of the case made by the Office of Special Plans that he angrily confronted Dick Cheney, flung the playbook's pages in the air, and yelled, "I'm not reading this bullshit!" But the good general did read it before the U.N. General Assembly within a matter of days. Asked about the duplicity of his old friend Powell, Zinni replied, "He's trying to be the good soldier, and I respect him for that." A month later, on January 8, 2004, Powell conceded that despite his assertions to the contrary before the United Nations, there was nothing solid to tie in Saddam with bin Laden and al-Qaida, which would have connected Iraq to the war on terrorism. "I have not seen smoking gun, concrete evidence about the connection," he answered in response to a press question. "But I think the possibility of such a connection did exist, and it was prudent to consider them at the time that we did." But the good soldier said nothing about whether he thought it might have been prudent to have smoking-gun evidence before going ahead rather than deceive the American people about a casus belli.

During Campaign 2000, Bush adopted the foreign policy of his father: multilateralism rather than unilateralism, negotiation and international concert rather than preemptive strikes. But once in power, his policy abruptly changed as the ideologues took over. From the start, National Security Advisor Condoleezza Rice, an academic who had specialized in anti-Soviet screeds while with the conservative Hoover Institution at Stanford, was assigned to craft a unilateral policy. As early as July 2001, two months before the 9/11 attacks, she announced, "Saddam Hussein is on the radar screen for the administration." Paul O'Neill, Bush's first secretary of the Treasury who concurrently sat on the National Security Council, revealed in January 2004 on *CBS News*, "From the very beginning there was a conviction that Saddam Hussein was a bad person and that he needed to go." At National Security Council meetings no one questioned why Iraq should be invaded. "It was all about finding a way to do it," O'Neill said. "That was the tone of it. The president saying, 'Go find me a way to do this.'" But O'Neill never saw anything about WMD in Iraq that "would rise to the level of evidence." The 9/11 attacks provided the opportunity. In *Bush at War*, Bob Woodward disclosed that only four days after the attacks top officials were brainstorming ways and means of getting rid of Saddam.

What they did was merge the assault against Saddam into the war on terrorism against bin Laden in the public mind. And that strategy, according to an Army War College report published in January 2004, boomeranged. The report, written by Professor Jeffrey Record, who is on the faculty of the Air War College, accused the Bush administration of detouring into an "unnecessary" war in Iraq and pursuing an "unrealistic" quest against terrorism that may lead to American wars with states that pose no serious threat. The report concluded that Iraq, which did not present a threat, "was a war-of-choice distraction from the war-of-necessity against" al-Qaida. "[The] global war on terrorism as currently defined and waged is dangerously indiscriminate and ambitious, and accordingly . . . its parameters should be readjusted." The antiterrorism campaign, the report summed up, "is strategically unfocused, promises more than it can deliver, and threatens to dissipate U.S. military resources in an endless and hopeless search for absolute security." The thrust of the Army War College report is that the war on terrorism is not subject to a military solution.

Which reverts to General Zinni's judgment that the Bush administration "screwed up" on Iraq, and his suggestion that Bush himself had been "captured" by the neocon ideologues in his

Cabinet and their top aides. It is not difficult to imagine how he was taken over by the older, wiser and more scheming Cheney and his chums. Bush was a foreign policy naïf, his gullibility put on exhibit early in his presidency when he afforded Russian President Vladimir Putin the special privilege of a visit to his Crawford ranch. Bush turned on his Texas charm, afterward telling reporters he had "looked into his [Putin's] eyes and saw sincerity there," intimating that they had bonded like old buddies. As it turned out, Putin had picked his pocket: the ex-KGB officer resolutely opposed Bush's rump invasion of Iraq. But, as Wolfowitz attested, Bush had oil on his mind. Perhaps because of his limited intellect and verbal infirmities, he chose to identify himself as a Crawford cowboy instead of an Ivy League elite. He is obsessed with playing commander in chief, perhaps out of a psychological need due to his Vietnam War avoidance (as one military veteran put it, calling George Bush "macho" is like calling Liberace "slugger"). Paul O'Neill lampooned that at meetings he was "like a blind man in a room full of deaf people," saying Bush was disengaged and gave top aides "little more than hunches about what the president might think." What O'Neill was witnessing was a chief executive who, oddly, doesn't read newspapers, and makes decisions, as he told Bob Woodward, based on his gut instincts. All of which convinced his handlers that his public appearances had to be carefully scripted, with little opportunity for spontaneity. Even his proposal for manned flights to the moon and Mars, an election-year booster shot to national pride, originated with Cheney (Bush avoided mentioning the cost, an estimated $400 billion and up).

His infrequent press conferences with the pool of reporters covering the White House are choreographed to prevent the dreaded slip of the tongue. In the June 2003 *Vanity Fair*, James Wolcott described a press conference on March 6, 2003, as Bush was about to lead the nation to war:

> It was a solemn, hollow piece of absurdist theater. Members of the press were marched into the room two by two like schoolchildren on a field trip to the planetarium. Departing from precedent, the president refused to entertain a random volley of questions; instead, he chose reporters from a prepared list, the resulting colloquy so stilted that he couldn't resist blurting out at one embarrassing juncture that the entire evening was "scripted." As Matt Taibbi explained in a damning column in the *New York Press*, the White House press corps collaborated in this charade, behaving as if they were being operated by remote control. "In other words," he wrote, "not only were reporters going out of their way to make sure their softballs were pre-approved, but they even went so far as to act on Bush's behalf, raising their hands and jockeying in their seats to better give the appearance of a spontaneous news conference."

But the plastic president can become nastily animated on the occasion—and it is seldom—when a reporter doesn't lob a softball question that he can hit out of the park. Take the case of Helen Thomas, who for forty years, ever since the heady days of President Kennedy, has been a White House correspondent, most of the time for UPI, recently for the Hearst syndicate. Now in her early eighties, Thomas has a reputation as a waspish, dogged questioner who has been treated with annoyed respect by the succession of presidents, including the elder George Bush. Through courtesy and tradition, Thomas long ago was awarded a front-row seat at the press conferences, but now she is shunned like a bag lady who has slipped past security. Thomas, something of a celebrity herself, had committed the mortal sin of expressing, to an interviewer, the informed opinion that George W. Bush was the worst president in American history, allowing that there was always the possibility of redemption. That put her on the White House enemies list. At the next press conference, which was the one before the Iraq session, Bush heaped scorn on her. As James Wolcott told it, "[He] responded to a query from Thomas about the separation of church and state with a Method actor's battery of mannerisms; the camera recorded him staring, twitching, pursing his lips, and at one point nearly crossing his eyes like Anthony Perkins at the end of *Psycho*. When she presumed to interrupt his platitudinous reply, he said with a cobra smile, 'I didn't get to finish my answer, in all due respect.'" After that Thomas became a press unperson, denied her customary seat, her raised hand ignored. The press conferences returned to sterility.

But hell hath no fury like a Bush scorned by an insider. The White House demands blind loyalty from its personnel, which is a way of saying it is the most secretive and hermetic administration in modern history. Not even Richard Nixon, who drew the blinds on the Watergate burglaries, was as averse to daylight. The only outfit I can compare it with is J. Edgar Hoover's FBI. In practically every field office there hung a framed print taken from Elbert Hubbard's "Get Out or Get in Line": "If you work for a man, for heaven's sake work for him! If he pays you wages that supply your bread and butter, work for him—speak well of him, think well of him, stand by him, and stand by the institution he represents." Agents knew it as Hoover's loyalty oath, a conformity command.

But I decided that there was a transcending loyalty to country, that it was in the interest of public safety to inform Congress how a public agency discharged its public trust. I wrote letters to Congress exposing the cult of personality surrounding Hoover, his default on combating organized crime in favor of tilting at the Red windmill. Time would vindicate my stand, but the immediate effect was character assassination by Hoover hatchet men that ostracized me from the job market. Even years later, when I was appointed to the joint presidential-congressional National Wiretap Commission that probed how anti-electronic eavesdropping laws were working, the FBI tried (unsuccessfully) to get me kicked off.

The Bush administration's reaction to perceived disloyalty exceeds even Hoover's in vindictiveness. Ambassador Joseph Wilson was asked to go to Africa, where he had contacts, to check out a report Cheney had received that Niger shipped "yellowcake" uranium to Iraq, the implication being that Saddam was developing a nuclear capacity. Wilson returned with the bad news that there was nothing to it. In fact, a postdated Niger government document that talked about such shipments turned out to be a crude forgery. Nevertheless, Bush used the canard, attributing it to the British, in his 2003 State of the Union speech preparing the nation for war. After the war, when Bush continued to cite the uranium story as justification for the invasion, Wilson was sickened by the continued deception of the American public. He wrote an op-ed piece in the *New York Times* setting the record straight. Nine days later the empire struck back. Conservative columnist Robert Novak, quoting "two senior administration officials," outed Wilson's wife, Valerie Plame, as a clandestine CIA "operative on weapons of mass destruction." It was a concerted effort — three other newspaper journalists received identical leaks. A felony crime had been committed in the White House, a violation of the federal law forbidding disclosure of the identity of an undercover operative. Plame had been running a NOK (not to our knowledge) operation in the Middle East. The retaliation put her life at risk as well as the lives of her undercover agents, and exposed the cover company out of which they were operating. Instead of vowing to identify and prosecute the guilty, Bush prophesied, "We may never know." Since there are only a handful of senior officials, the list of suspects should have been short. But after months on the case, the FBI had not gotten its man — or men. If agents had polygraphed Dick Cheney, who had dispatched Wilson to Africa in the first place, and Karl Rove, a longtime Novak source, they weren't saying.

Bush must have been especially ticked at the "disloyalty" of Paul O'Neill, the ultimate insider. From day one, O'Neill regularly attended Cabinet meetings with the president, as well as those of the National Security Council of which he was an ex officio member. He was secretary of the Treasury, through the 9/11 attacks, for nearly two years. He told his story in *The Price of Loyalty: George W. Bush, the White House and the Education of Paul O'Neill,* written by Pulitzer Prize–winning journalist Ron Susskind. In O'Neill's account, Cheney, with whom he served in the Ford administration, looms large. As *Time* for January 19, 2004, put it after interviewing O'Neill, "The incurious President was so opaque on some important issues that Cabinet officials were left guessing his mind even after face-to-face meetings. Cheney is portrayed as an unstoppable force, unbowed by inconvenient facts as he drives Administration policy toward his goals." O'Neill absolutely shatters the image of Bush as a strong, decisive leader. "From his first meeting with the president," *Time* wrote, "O'Neill found Bush unengaged and inscrutable, an inside account far different than the shiny White House brochure version of an unfailing leader questioning aides with rapid-fire intensity." After the 2002 elections, O'Neill, noted for his straight talk on a planet of bureauspeak, told his old comrade Cheney that increasing budget deficits threatened the economy. Cheney cut him off. "Reagan proved deficits don't matter," he said. "We won the midterms. This is our due." O'Neill was dumbfounded at such a raw exercise of political power. A few weeks later Cheney was on the phone. "Paul, the President has decided to make some changes

in the economic team," he led off, "and you're part of the change."
Cheney requested him to announce that it was O'Neill's decision
to leave Washington to return to private life. O'Neill refused, retort-
ing, "I'm too old to begin telling lies now."

But it was the Iraq part of *The Price of Loyalty*—the book was
published on the day the 500th GI was killed in Iraq—that sent the
White House ballistic. "From the start, we were building the case
against Hussein and looking at how we could take him out and
change Iraq into a new country," O'Neill said. "And, if we did that,
it would solve everything. It was about finding a way to do it." To be
precise, O'Neill pinpointed the very first Cabinet meeting as when
the deposition of Saddam first was discussed, and that topped the
day's agenda. This put the lie to the administration's posture that
the removal of Saddam was only prioritized after 9/11, when it was
presented to the American people as an integral part of the war on
terrorism, not a separate objective.

The opening volley against O'Neill was fired by an anonymous
administration official who was quoted as saying, "No one listened
to his wacky ideas when he was in office. Why should we start now?"
Then it was announced that the Treasury Department's inspector
general would investigate whether any of the 19,000 pages of documents on a CD-ROM that O'Neill took with him when he left office, and to which Susskind had access, were classified, but that
only broadcast the news that the book was thoroughly documented.
Bush, speaking from Mexico where he was attending an intra-Ameri-
cas conference, lamely claimed he was only continuing the Clinton
administration's "regime change" policy. In truth, Clinton had no
plans for an invasion, and worked within the U.N. framework. His
national security advisor, Sandy Berger, was able to separate Iraq
from the war on terrorism. O'Neill was surprised at the fury of the

White House reaction to his bombshell disclosure, since he had approved of ousting Saddam. But he was resolute. "I'm an old guy, and I'm rich," he told *Time*. "And there's nothing they can do to hurt me."

O'Neill's narrative reinforces General Anthony Zinni's conviction that the neocons have taken control of the Bush administration, or "captured" the president, as Zinni puts it. The former Cabinet member experienced Bush as "unengaged" and "inscrutable," while the archneocon Cheney was into everything, an "unstoppable force" who was "unbowed by inconvenient facts as he drives Administration policy toward his goals."

Acknowledging that he made a mistake in endorsing Bush-Cheney in 2000, Zinni gave a signature speech in September 2003 to hundreds of Marine and Navy officers and others in a suburban Virginia ballroom. "My contemporaries, our feelings and sensitivities were forged on the battlefields of Vietnam, where we heard the garbage and the lies, and we saw the sacrifice," he said. "I ask you, is it happening again?" The speech, delivered at a forum sponsored by the Marine Corps Association and U.S. Naval Institute, drew prolonged applause, with many officers standing.

Zinni told reporter Ricks that he hasn't received a single negative response from military people about the stance he has taken. "I was surprised by the number of uniformed guys, all ranks, who said, 'You're speaking for us. Keep on keeping on.'"

10

MISSION LOST

On January 15, 2004, only days after acknowledging he was "warming up" for Campaign 2004, a beaming George W. Bush stood before the cameras at NASA headquarters to formally announce a long-range project to send manned space vehicles to the moon and then on to Mars. "We will build new ships to carry man forward into the universe," he said, looking every bit the visionary.

In juxtaposition, that same night the shadow president, Dick Cheney, grimly gave a major address on the war on terrorism before the World Affairs Council in Los Angeles that made Bush look like a lightweight. In a doomsday scenario, Cheney warned of the growing threat of a catastrophic terrorist attack in the United States. "Instead of losing thousands of lives," he said, "we might lose tens or even hundreds of thousands of lives as a result of a single attack, or a set of coordinated attacks." Cheney, oblivious to Bush's recent Pollyanna statements that progress was being made in the war on terrorism, painted a bleak picture of a resurgent, expanded, globe-girdling al-Qaida. "Scattered in more than fifty nations, the al-Qaida network and other terrorist groups constitute an enemy unlike any other that we have ever faced," he declared. "And as our intelligence shows, the terrorists continue plotting to kill on an ever-larger scale, including here in the United States." Cheney said the administration was embarked on a military solution to the threat, expanding the armed forces into even more overseas bases so the United States could wage lightning wars around the world. "One of the legacies of this administration will be some of the most sweeping changes in our military, and our national security strategy as it relates to the military and force structure, and how we're based, and how we used it in the last fifty or sixty years, probably since World War II." Cheney envisioned endless wars.

The Bush-Cheney presentations were delivered just as the 500th American soldier was about to die on the killing field of Iraq, a pace that matched that of the Vietnam War circa 1965.

The Cheney plan is structurally flawed because it deploys a conventional military response to counter an unconventional threat. Cheney correctly characterized al-Qaida and its confederate groups as a network, not a nation, which ordinarily would suggest that the CIA be in charge, not the Pentagon. After all, the invasion of Iraq had nothing to do with the war on terrorism. If armies could crush terrorism, Israel would be the safest place in the world. But Cheney tipped off his hidden agenda when he warned that only an administration of proven ability could manage the dramatic overhaul necessary. Cheney has conjured up a terrorist bogeyman of epic proportions both in scope and duration, terrorizing the American people into believing that only Bush and Cheney stand between them and a plague of cataclysmic events. It was a tactic that J. Edgar Hoover used to perpetuate himself in power over several decades;

he portrayed himself as the nation's indispensable defender against a communist takeover.

The godfather of the neocon movement, Cheney has taken aim at nothing less than a neocon takeover through perpetual emergency. In the wake of the First Gulf War, which failed to dislodge Saddam, he retreated to a Montana hunting lodge and drafted a manifesto that was eventually formalized into the Project for the New American Century (PNAC). The current PNAC manifesto, written in September 2000 in anticipation of a Bush election victory, called for a quantum leap in military spending, the establishment of American armed forces bases in strategic areas, abrogation of noisome international treaties, hegemony over global energy resources, militarization of outer space, and the option to use nuclear weapons to obtain American goals, presaging a renewed arms race. The defense industry and companies like Cheney's Halliburton and the senior Bush's Carlyle Group stand to reap windfall profits from this doctrine. If Cheney gets his way, the two-party system in America will effectively be no more. Implanted fears and endless wars will keep the Republicans in power. And the neocons will control the Republican administration, as they do now.

Although Bush is widely perceived as a decisive leader, the record shows that he has badly mismanaged the war on terrorism. In the months leading up to the 9/11 attacks, there is no evidence that he assigned a high priority to the menace of al-Qaida even though the playbook passed down from Clinton national security advisor Sandy Berger did. Instead of focusing on al-Qaida, Condoleezza Rice was preoccupied with fashioning a unilateral foreign policy. And Attorney General John Ashcroft, who was responsible for the FBI, was so driven by his religious zealotry that he was busy trying to stamp out interstate pornography. Bush's myopia led him to ignore the neon sign that lit up on August 6, 2001, at his Crawford ranch when Rice gave him a CIA briefing that al-Qaida was planning to hijack airliners and crash them into buildings. This as it turned out was al-Qaida's resolve to finish the job on the World Trade Center that it had started years earlier with a truck bomb. But Bush took no action. What other missteps Bush made in failing to prevent 9/11 are the subject of a probe by the National Commission on Terrorist Attacks Upon the United States, which is also assessing the performance of the intelligence agencies before and after the attacks. Bush didn't want the commission established in the first place—accountability is not one of his strong suits—but finally bowed to pressure brought by the families of the 9/11 victims. In October 2003 the commission chairman, former New Jersey governor Thomas Keane, expressed frustration at Bush's stalling on furnishing documents, in particular the daily intelligence reports known as the Presidential Daily Briefings. "I will not stand for it," Keane said. "That means we will use every tool at our command to get hold of every document." A member of the panel, former senator Max Cleland, complained that the White House stalling tactics meant that chances were dim the commission could complete its work before a statutory deadline in May 2004. "It's obvious that the White House wants to run out the clock here," he said. He asserted that the Bush administration feared what the commission was uncovering. "As each day goes by," Cleland disclosed, "we learn that this government knew a whole lot more about these terrorists before September 11 than it has ever admitted."

Bush began losing the war on terrorism three days after 9/11 when, at the urgent request of the Saudi Arabian ambassador, Prince Bandar, an old friend of the Bush family, he instructed the FBI to chaperone out of the United States members of the bin Laden family and the House of Saud, the Saudi royals. At the time, the country was a no-fly zone, but Saudi-chartered airliners were able to hopscotch in and out of cities picking up the Saudis and flying them back to the desert kingdom. The move stymied the FBI from questioning them about money trails to al-Qaida, a subject on which they were presumed to have some knowledge. Why did Bush jeopardize national security to grant a Saudi request? In an interview in *Rolling Stone* on January 5, 2004, titled "The House of Bush," longtime Republican strategist Kevin Phillips articulates the ties that bind: "By the time George W. came in, he was the product of a family that was more embroiled in the Mid East than almost any other American family—to say nothing of any other major American political family. The administration has not been interested in turning over any rocks that represent Saudi Arabia, because the Bush family has been in bed with them for so long."

At first, in his Wild West way, Bush announced he was going to "git" Osama bin Laden and bring him back dead or alive. He sent an expeditionary force to Afghanistan and defeated the Taliban militia that reputedly was protecting bin Laden and his high command. But he didn't round up bin Laden, who was thought to be holed up in the mountain fastness near the Pakistani border, and within months was declaring his quarry "not important" and moving on to Iraq. A heavy price has been paid for not finishing business in Afghanistan. Today the puppet president of the country rules only in Kabul; the provinces belong to whoever has a gun. The Taliban and al-Qaida are resurgent, and fighting has flared with the token American force, whose death toll now exceeds one hundred. So much for Bush's nation building.

But Afghanistan didn't have oil reserves rivaling those of Saudi

Arabia. It was Iraq that had been on the neocons' drawing board since 1998, their dream war. So it was decided to seize the opportunity of using the war on terrorism as a cover for invasion. The key justification floated was that Saddam was acquiring a nuclear capability, raising the specter of a nuclear attack on the United States. In his 2003 State of the Union speech, which laid the groundwork for war, Bush claimed, citing British intelligence sources, that Saddam had tried to buy uranium from an unnamed African country. What he didn't say was that his own intelligence services had downgraded the report as questionable. After the war, when Ambassador Joseph Wilson blew the whistle on the claim, Bush moved to clear himself of telling a big lie. He commissioned an in-house group that he had appointed, the Foreign Intelligence Advisory Board, to look into the matter. Their conclusion, leaked to the press, was that there was "no deliberate effort to fabricate," simply an eagerness "to grab onto something affirmative" about Hussein's nuclear ambitions. Left out was any judgment about the ethic of going to war based on eagerness.

On December 21, 2003, Walter Pincus of the *Washington Post* posed the question of who lied if it wasn't Bush. "One enduring mystery," he wrote, "is which White House official was responsible for promoting the material in question." The chief suspect was Dick Cheney. He was the one in the White House most passionately promoting the war. He was the one who had repeatedly visited CIA headquarters trying to wheedle analysts into putting a WMD spin on their reports. He was the one who had dispatched Ambassador Wilson to Africa on a mission that backfired. And he was the one who, as General Zinni put it, had "captured" George Bush.

It is clear now that the Bush administration badly miscalculated the reception that awaited from the Iraqi people. An article by George

Packer in *The New Yorker* of November 24, 2003, entitled "War After the War" is illuminating on that score. Planning for postwar Iraq was undertaken by Wolfowitz's chief deputy at the Pentagon, Douglas Feith, the same Feith who had used his recondite shop, the Office of Special Plans, to spin a web of fabrications in justification of the war. The secretary of the army at the time, Thomas E. White, told Packer that Feith's team "had the mind-set that this would be a relatively straightforward, manageable task, because this would be a war of liberation, and therefore the reconstruction would be short-lived."

This was the view held by exiles in the Iraqi National Congress led by Ahmad Chalabi, who told Bush that Iraqis would receive their liberators with "sweets and flowers." Cheney and Wolfowitz stated publicly that the cost of reconstruction would be covered by Iraqi oil revenue. By the time he made his May Day "Mission Accomplished" landing on the aircraft carrier, Bush had requested only $2.4 billion for postwar rebuilding. By the time he materialized at the Baghdad airport on Thanksgiving for a photo op with a turkey, the number had shot up to $87 billion and counting. It was sticker shock for Congress, which, having been deceived into endorsing the war to begin with, had no alternative but to pay it.

There is no end in sight for the war after the war. The capture of Saddam made no difference in the tempo of the insurgency that was killing American troops and Iraqis seen as collaborators. If anything, the intensity picked up. This was undoubtedly due to the advent in Iraq of a jihadist cadre called the Mujahedi al-Salafiyah who practice Salafism, a fanatical brand of Sunni Islam that was ruthlessly suppressed by Saddam. *Time* magazine on January 26, 2004, reported on its interview of a cell leader: "The man, who goes by the nom de guerre Abu Ali, says the Salafists model themselves on the mujahedin who drove the Soviets out of Afghanistan in the 1980s and on other jihad movements."

On the political front, turmoil continued. Cheney and Wolfowitz flew in Chalabi and his exile entourage as soon as Saddam's statue was toppled, figuring he would be "our man in Baghdad," who would run the country in their image and likeness. But Chalabi had been gone so long he had no constituency, and the transitional Iraqi Governing Council to which he belonged was perceived as packed with American appointees. Opposition factions strongly objected to a plan by the American proconsul L. Paul Bremer to hold provincial caucuses rather than free elections, seeing it as a ploy to install candidates favored by the occupation authorities. The whole farrago came to a boil on January 18, 2004, when a powerful truck bomb exploded at the main entrance to Bremer's Coalition Provisional Authority, killing 24 and injuring another 120. The following day a huge Shi'ite crowd, estimated in the tens of thousands, marched in Baghdad in support of the revered Grand Ayatollah Ali al-Sistani, who called for early direct elections. Since Shi'ite Muslims account for some 60 percent of the population, it was an ominous message that a powerful force would not stand for an American puppet regime. Desperate for political reasons to turn over governance to the Iraqis by June 30—it was an election year—the Bush administration practically begged Kofi Annan, whom it had stiffed in the run-up to war, to send U.N. experts to resolve the voting issue. The political scene in Iraq promised to remain volatile into the foreseeable future, requiring the continued presence of American troops. A secular state under Saddam, Iraq was boding to devolve into a radical Muslim theocracy. This eventuality would add nothing to the stability of the region. Nor to the profits of Halliburton.

In an audiotape aired October 19, 2003, a voice believed by the

CIA to be that of Osama bin Laden promised suicide attacks "inside and outside" the United States, and threatened nations helping in the occupation of Iraq. Addressing American troops as if they were mercenaries, bin Laden said, "Your blood will be spilled so the White House gang gets richer and the arms dealers with them, as well as the large companies involved." The jeremiad signaled that al-Qaida was reinvigorated after Bush declared bin Laden "not important" and took a sabbatical from the war on terrorism to invade Iraq. Given a window of opportunity, al-Qaida and its newfound allies took on a global cast with bin Laden in an emeritus role. Now if he is killed or captured, he will be an inspirational martyr to the network. And al-Qaida, reinforced by new blood and buoyed by the sympathy of millions of more Muslims radicalized by Bush's war on Iraq, will keep on its deadly mission.

The backlash to the Iraq war can be seen in Saudi Arabia of all places. Writing in *The New Yorker* on January 5, 2004, Lawrence Wright, a newspaperman temporarily in the kingdom to mentor apprentice journalists, reported that public opinion was overwhelmingly against the invasion. Wright said:

> On March 23rd, the front page of the *Gazette* showed an Iraqi child with his head blown off. The Arabic press and many of the satellite channels framed the bombing of Baghdad as "America's war on children." The lens of Al Jazeera focused on Iraqis kneeling in front of the coalition troops with their hands behind their heads; it was a war designed to humiliate the Arabs once again. The Wahhabi clerics ranted against the infidels. "The Crusaders have come to take over!" one imam in Jeddah intoned in a sermon. The Saudi public was understandably inflamed.

One of the relentless themes of the Saudi media was that the twin objects of American power were oil and murder. Although the Saudi government soon ordered the media to drop its anti-American line, the invasion had turned the Saudi people against Bush and set the stage for al-Qaida. On May 12 indigenous al-Qaida units bombed three Riyadh housing compounds occupied by foreigners, killing thirty-four, including Americans. A subsequent bombing in November killed eighteen. There followed frequent raids and shoot-outs with suspected terrorists. Police said that al-Qaida was gunning for the royal family. Should an assassination attack succeed, Saudi Arabia might well fall into the hands of the extreme fundamentalist Wahhabi clerics.

Another strategic country in jeopardy due to invasion blowback is Pakistan, a hotbed of strong anti-American feelings. Following the 9/11 attacks, the United States persuaded President Pervez Musharraf to help in the next-door campaign against the Taliban. By turning on the Taliban, allowing American forces to use Pakistani territory as a springboard to Afghanistan, Musharraf surrounded himself with domestic enemies. Elements of his army and intelligence service are partial to the Taliban and al-Qaida. Muslim extremism is on the rise since the unprovoked assault on Iraq. Indigenous terrorist groups have banded together under the umbrella of the United Muslim Army, the better to coordinate attacks on Western interests. And Musharraf himself has been targeted. In September 2003, Osama bin Laden's top deputy, Dr. Ayman Zawahiri, released an audiotape exhorting followers to overthrow Musharraf for his collaboration with the Americans. Shortly thereafter, on December 14, the Pakistani leader narrowly escaped with his life when terrorists blew up a bridge he had just crossed, and eleven days later a suicide driver rammed his motorcade, missing him but killing sixteen others. If the terrorists eventually succeed in assassinating Musharraf, the possibility of a radical Islamic regime succeeding him lurks. What makes this scenario alarming is that Pakistan possesses a nuclear capacity, the so-called Islamic bomb.

So by arousing the sleeping giant of Arab nationalism, Bush has destabilized the Middle East. Yet such was his hubris that only two months after the fall of Baghdad he thought he was such a hero in the region that he could step in and—voilà!—solve the Israeli-Palestinian impasse. While it provided a photo op of him flanked by a representative from each side stepping across a "bridge over troubled waters," his touted "Road Map for Peace" turned out to be just another slogan. One of the problems, according to *New York Times* columnist Thomas L. Friedman, writing on August 4, 2003, was "the massive passive support for Osama bin Laden" in the Arab world.

No sooner had Bush declared victory in the truncated war against Iraq than high explosives went off around the world like a string of firecrackers, punctuating the resurgence of al-Qaida. But his haughty derision of France and Germany after they were unwilling to join his "coalition of the willing," his petty snubbing of Jacques Chirac and Gerhardt Schroeder, alienated two key players in the worldwide counterintelligence thrust against al-Qaida and its allies. At home and abroad, Bush is a divider, not a uniter, which is to al-Qaida's advantage.

At home, Secretary Tom Ridge of the superbureacracy Department of Homeland Security wants you to know that you're in safe hands with him. This despite the fact that almost three years after 9/11, only 5 percent of the ocean cargo entering U.S. ports is inspected for WMD parts or assemblies. This despite the clumsy countermeasures he continued to introduce. In reaction to the 2003 Christmas al-Qaida hobgoblin, during which a number of international flights were canceled, he ruled that every foreign airliner landing at airports in this country has to have armed marshals on board, which raised the point that if it was such a good idea, why wasn't it thought of years earlier? Another Ridge brainstorm was the photographing and fingerprinting of foreigners arriving at U.S. airports, a device to keep better track of when visitors enter and leave. But in an act of profiling countries, Ridge decreed that visitors from twenty-eight nations, mostly European, were exempt. This provoked a Bronx cheer in Brazil, which promptly started mugging and printing American visitors. Undeterred, Ridge came up with the loopy idea that when a passenger makes a reservation, the airline filters the data, including credit card number, through a federal watch-list computer so that upon arrival at the airport the passenger meets a color-coded reception: green for okay to fly; yellow for caution, question thoroughly; and red for stop. Held for questioning on one canceled Air France flight were a five-year-old boy with the same name as a suspected Tunisian terrorist, an elderly Chinese woman and a Welsh insurance agent. The government's dossier bank must be bulging—J. Edgar Hoover would be envious. But any self-respecting terrorist would, after 9/11, travel with a "clean" alias.

Ridge's feel-good utterances are irresponsible—the Department of Homeland Security cannot possibly stop another well-designed terrorist attack. That is the province of the counterintelligence arm of the FBI. But for some arcane reason, Bush has left the Bureau untouched in the face of its demonstrable flaws. It missed signals that might have averted 9/11—Zacarias Moussaoui is the most glaring example. It has continued to show its lack of smarts by such nonsense as circulating a memo to police departments telling them to be on the lookout for anyone with an almanac on the theory that the person might be a terrorist seeking data on the country's infrastructure. The Bureau's disqualifying affliction is a bipolar disorder —conflicted as to whether it is a law enforcement agency or counterintelligence agency. Senator John Edwards of the Intelligence Committee and other concerned members of Congress advocated that homeland counterintelligence—rooting out terrorist sleeper cells—be spun off into a new, independent agency designed specifically for the task. But Bush nixed the measure. So in an era of new challenges, we are stuck with the same old FBI.

As if conceding that the FBI wasn't up to the task of using democratic techniques, John Ashcroft came out swinging wildly at the Constitution and the Bill of Rights. It speaks volumes about the direction of his moral compass that he would permit the totalitarian tactic of torture by proxy, which he cloaks in the disguise of "extraordinary rendition." In an essay in the anthology *The War on Our Freedoms*, *New York Times* columnist Anthony Lewis struck back:

> The war on terrorism is being waged against a hidden enemy who is not going to surrender in a ceremony aboard the U.S.S. Missouri. The fear of terrorism may well go on for the rest of our lives. We may not have breathing space to understand and regret punitive excesses. If we are to preserve constitutional values— the values of freedom—understanding and resistance must come now. . . . The claim of executive power is at the heart of the matter. There has been no more sweeping claim, in living memory, than the Bush administration's assertions of power to hold any American in detention forever, without a trial and without access to counsel, simply by declaring him to be an enemy combatant.

But, you say, it can't happen to me. Think about the case of Luigi Garafano, as reported on *NBC News* on January 21, 2004. Garafano had been living in the United States for decades, raising a family, a model citizen. On November 4, 2003, as he returned from a pleasure trip to Italy, he was arrested by the Department of Homeland

Security and ordered deported. What triggered the whole thing was a minor drug conviction forty years in Garafano's past, long before George W. Bush ceased snorting cocaine. When a federal judge overturned the order on the grounds that there was absolutely no evidence Garafano was a wannabe terrorist, Ashcroft instructed his Justice Department attorneys to appeal. For Garafano, it was straight out of Kafka. For the rest of us, it is an object lesson in the Bush administration's utter contempt for individual rights in its reckless pursuit of phantom terrorists.

Why does Bush, who signs the torture-by-proxy fiats, go along with Ashcroft? Veteran Republican insider Kevin Phillips, who designed Nixon's Southern Strategy, which served the GOP for decades, thinks the Bushes are unprincipled. In his book *American Dynasty*, Phillips unloads: "Four generations of building toward dynasty have infused the Bush family's hunger for power and practices of crony capitalism with a moral arrogance and backstage disregard of the democratic and republican traditions of the U.S. government." As a result, he says, "deceit and disinformation have become Bush political hallmarks."

Bush's State of the Union address on January 20, 2003, provided a tableau of his intentions regarding the war on terrorism. Flanking him on his left was House Speaker Dennis Hastert, a pliable Republican who shut the door on the 9/11 Commission's probe of what the administration knew in advance about the al-Qaida plot. Hastert simply—and arbitrarily—refused to grant the commission a time extension to complete its work. Flanking him on his right was die-hard Dick Cheney, who stubbornly refused to accept the Army War College report that Iraq "was a war-of-choice distraction from the war-of-necessity against al Qaeda." A few days later Cheney would again promote the legend that Saddam had operational ties to al-

Qaida, which had been rebutted by Colin Powell that he had "not seen smoking-gun, concrete evidence." And Cheney would flog the dead horse that Saddam had WMD programs, saying, "We've found a couple of semi-trailers at this point which we believe were part of a program. I would deem that conclusive evidence, if you will, that he did in fact have programs for weapons of mass destruction." Surely he jested. The semi-trailers in question were used to generate hydrogen gas for artillery-spotter balloons sold by the British to Iraq years ago. Shortly thereafter, David Kay, head of the CIA's Iraq Survey Group scouring the country for evidence of WMD ever since Baghdad fell, quit his post because he found none. Kay blamed a "failure of intelligence," meaning the CIA, for the canard that there were WMD. The lie had come full circle: It was Cheney who had twisted the CIA's arm to come up with a WMD invention.

In his blustery State of the Union speech, Bush did not apologize for deceiving the American people about WMD. He did not mention the GI death toll in Iraq since his splashy landing on the *Abraham Lincoln* to proclaim the war effectively over, nor did he invite families of the dead for a ritual introduction. He retroactively justified the Iraq war on humanitarian grounds, saying Saddam's "torture chambers would still be filled with victims" but leaving unsaid how many torture-by-proxy warrants he himself signed. He referred to his nemesis, Osama bin Laden, only obliquely, noting it was "over two years without an attack on American soil, and it is tempting to believe that the danger is behind us." But he said, "That hope is understandable, comforting and false." The fact is that the 9/11 attacks were four years in the making by al-Qaida, and it is simply a matter of when, not if, the next Big One hits.

Trust me, I'm your commander in chief, Bush implored the American people in promising to protect them from terrorism.

How can you trust a commander in chief who once, in a drunken rage, threatened to punch out his own father?

How can you trust a commander in chief who lacked the courage to fight in the Vietnam War, which he schemed to avoid even though he was all for it?

How can you trust a commander in chief who is covering up what he knew beforehand that might have averted the 9/11 attacks?

How can you trust a commander in chief who kissed off Osama bin Laden as "not important" and moved on to an unnecessary invasion of Iraq, allowing al-Qaida to regroup and become stronger than ever?

How can you trust a commander in chief who thinks the war against an invisible enemy like al-Qaida can be won by generals with bombers, tanks and troops?

How can you trust a commander in chief whose failure to drastically overhaul an outmoded FBI compromises the public safety?

How can you trust a commander in chief who shirks responsibility for the artificial claim that Saddam was receiving uranium shipments from Africa by blaming the CIA, thus gutting morale at an agency that is critical to the real war on terrorism?

In short, mission *not* accomplished.

11

BANNERGATE

It must have been a moment of dread for George W. Bush in January 2004 when David Kay, his chief arms inspector, abruptly resigned as head of the Iraq Survey Group searching for WMD and went before Congress to testify that there were no biological or chemical weapons, no nuclear weapons and no connection with al-Qaida. Nor was there any evidence that the Iraqis had sneaked any banned weapons into Syria, as the White House had intimated. "I'm personally convinced that there were not large stockpiles of newly produced weapons of mass destruction," Kay conceded. "We don't find the people, the documents or the physical plants if the production was going on."

Kay, who was highly respected and had an independent streak, had just shot down the president's series of declaratory statements leading up to the war that Saddam Hussein not only possessed a WMD arsenal but was on the verge of using it. In his 2003 State of the Union speech, Bush had used those now-infamous sixteen words, "The British government has learned that Saddam Hussein recently sought significant quantities of uranium from Africa," raising the specter of a nuclear capability. In his buildup to war, Bush indulged in the doomsday rhetoric that the United States "must not ignore the threat gathering against us. Facing clear evidence of peril, we cannot wait for the final proof—the smoking gun—that could come in the form of a mushroom cloud." Then, as the invasion was about to begin, Bush asserted that "intelligence gathered by this and other governments leaves no doubt that the Iraq regime continues to possess and conceal some of the most lethal weapons ever devised."

Until Kay's bombshell, Bush had taken the position that finding WMD was merely a matter of time, that the Iraq Survey Group was continuing on, thus putting the issue on ice until after the presidential election. The initial reaction of the White House to Kay was denial. Bush, Condoleezza Rice and Donald Rumsfeld pleaded for more time, while Dick Cheney cited the pair of trailers, the ones that had been purchased from the British to generate hydrogen gas to inflate artillery balloons, as "conclusive evidence" that Iraq "did, in fact, have programs for weapons of mass destruction." Joining the fire drill was CIA Director George Tenet, who in a hastily arranged address tried to have it both ways, admitting Iraq had not posed an "imminent threat," but mitigating that damage by saying, "When the facts on Iraq are all in, we will be neither completely right nor completely wrong." He made no reference to a February 2003 report by his own agency, as disclosed on *MSNBC News* on October 24, 2003, that stated: "We do not have any direct evidence that Iraq has used the period since [1998, when U.N. inspectors left] to reconstitute its Weapons of Mass Destruction programs," which in any case had not progressed past the theoretical stage. Nor did he allude to the earlier congressional testimony of the expert on chemical and biological weapons, Christian Westermann, that he felt pressured to alter his reports to square with the Bush administration's line.

Only Colin Powell broke ranks. In an interview by the *Washington Post* on February 3, 2004, Powell allowed that he was not sure he would have recommended an invasion had he known that Saddam did not have stockpiles of banned weapons. That, he said, "changes the political calculus" about whether to go to war. It was not the first time Powell was concerned about intelligence distortion: As recounted in *U.S. News & World Report* on June 9, 2003, when he read the first draft of his speech to the United Nations prepared by Dick Cheney's office he became so upset that he lost his temper, flinging pages in the air and fuming, "I'm not reading this. This is bullshit!" But of course when the time came, he did read it. So it went with the *Washington Post* departure from groupthink. By the next day, after Cheney administered a verbal spanking, Powell had shifted into reverse. "The bottom line is this," he said. "The president made the right decision."

Kay's testimony, however, had ignited a political firestorm. After all, if Bill Clinton's lying about sex was grounds for impeachment, what about a president who would lie to go to war? There were well over five hundred dead American soldiers, with the toll mounting, as well as an estimated fifteen thousand Iraqis, both civilian and military. Iraq had become a killing field with no end in sight. If al-Qaida had not been there before, they were now. With Senator John McCain calling for a congressional investigation, Bush took the play away by forming his own Iraq intelligence commission called the Commission on the Intelligence Capabilities of the United States Regarding Weapons of Mass Destruction. He named its members, and they would be accountable to him. Significantly, his first appointee was McCain, which put him inside Bush's tent rather than loose on the outside. But it was not to be a wide-ranging probe. Bush explained he was "determined to figure out why" some pre-war assessments of the Iraq threat have not been confirmed. If there was any doubt he feared the political fallout of even this circumscribed mandate, it vanished when he announced that the commission would not issue its final report until March 2005—well past the election. And to ensure that it stay on the straight and narrow, he named a personal friend of Dick Cheney, Judge Laurence Silberman, as cochairman.

Where Bush didn't want the commission to go was the question of what he knew about the failed intelligence when he made the case for war to the American people. The "failure" was that the CIA had not come up with any smoking-gun evidence of WMD because they didn't exist, yet he hyped raw reports into a mushroom cloud. But Bush couldn't put the genie back in the bottle on his signature claim that Saddam Hussein was receiving shipments of yellowcake uranium from Niger. Following his trip to Africa to look into it, Ambassador Joe Wilson had reported back to Dick Cheney the bad news that there had been no uranium shipments to Iraq—the whole thing was a fiction. But Bush didn't allow the truth to get in the way of a good story, even if it consisted of only sixteen words.

George W. Bush lied to the American people.

It was his Bannergate. That he had lost the war on terrorism became glaringly evident on March 11, 2004, when professionally synchronized bombings of three commuter trains in Madrid killed 202 and wounded 1500. It was three days before elections, and the government of Prime Minister Jose Maria Aznar, a right-winger who had ostentatiously supported Bush's unprovoked strike against Iraq despite the opposition of 90 percent of the people, was an odds-on favorite to win. Aznar stalled, blaming the carnage—it was called

Spain's 9/11 — on the indigenous Basque separatist group ETA. But within a day, evidence was found implicating an al-Qaida faction cell in Spain. Overnight Spaniards turned against Aznar, blaming his alliance with Bush for making Spain a target. In the voting, Aznar's party was emphatically removed from power. The new prime minister, Jose Luis Rodriguez Zapatero, promised to yank Spanish troops out of Iraq. "The war has been a disaster," he said. "The occupation continues to be a great disaster. It hasn't generated anything but more violence and hate."

Less than a week after the bombings in Spain, a 1000-pound car bomb cratered the Jabal Lebanon Hotel in central Baghdad, killing 17 and injuring 47. The time and place, on the eve of the first anniversary of the invasion behind Firdaus Square where U.S. soldiers had toppled a bronze statue of Saddam Hussein upon entering the city, were obviously intended to send the message that the insurgency had only begun. As American soldiers tried to enter the hotel site to help out, they were pushed back by angry Iraqis shouting, "We were better off under Saddam."

The double blasts punctuated Bush's mishandling of the war on terrorism. Early on, he abandoned the hunt for Osama bin Laden and his al-Qaida perpetrators of the 9/11 attacks, declaring bin Laden "not important." He diverted resources to an invasion of Iraq, which had nothing to do with 9/11 but had been the dream scene of Dick Cheney's neocon cabal since 1998. A U.S. Army War College report concluded that Iraq presented no threat, that it "was a war-of-choice distraction from the war-of-necessity against" al-Qaida. Yet Bush "justified" it by lying and distorting intelligence. When the lightning war unexpectedly morphed into a murderous quagmire, the Vietnam War wimp turned into a movie tough guy by taunting, "Bring 'em on." They came on, and Iraq remains a killing field.

The Iraq diversion gave bin Laden a window of opportunity to rejuvenate al-Qaida and expand its support base. The millions of new Muslim radicals and a hundred new bin Ladens predicted by Egyptian President Mubarak as the consequence of an attack on Iraq have joined in solidarity with their brothers around the world. Bin Laden became a mystic leader, not operational, so that his capture would make him a martyr. Dozens of terrorist groups have sprung up, CIA director George Tenet testified before Congress in February 2004, but he has only been able to identify a few of them. Tenet talked of "a global movement infected by al-Qaeda's radical agenda" and said "the steady growth of bin Laden's anti-American sentiment and the broad dissemination of al-Qaeda's destructive expertise ensure that a serious threat will remain for the foreseeable future, with or without al-Qaeda in the picture."

So Bush's politically motivated Iraq adventure has proliferated the terrorist threat worldwide. His arrogant demeaning of key allies in the war on terrorism, who flunked his loyalty test by refusing to join in his unprovoked war against Saddam Hussein because there was no credible evidence Iraq possessed WMD, has jeopardized international cooperation. Those countries who did join his pickup squad are fearful of retaliatory blowback such as happened in Spain. And Bush, who loves to strut in military garb, has yet to learn that conventional military force is useless against terrorism.

The irony is that Cheney's long-standing obsession with Iraq may have compromised prevention of the 9/11 attacks. NBC News correspondent Lisa Meyers revealed on March 18, 2004 that from the start Bush's national security team focused almost exclusively on Cheney's pet project to the virtual exclusion of the threat posed by al-Qaida. This held true even after the team was notified that al-Qaida was responsible for the bombing of the USS *Cole*. There were other missed signals, capped by a CIA briefing of Bush on August 6, 2001, at his Texas ranch that an al-Qaida plot was pending to hijack airliners and suicide-crash them into targeted buildings. (After 9/11 Bush admitted that he could not "envision" such a plot.) The Bush team did not become proactive on al-Qaida until two days before 9/11, when it authorized the CIA to use an Afghan asset to go after bin Laden. By that time it was too late.

George W. Bush is not part of the solution, he is part of the problem. Because of his decisions, the world is a much more dangerous place.

Index

FAREWELL AMERICA
The Plot to Kill JFK

by James Hepburn (a pseudonym)
Introduction by William Turner

This is a pungent historical document.
— *Publishers Weekly*

Paperback, 416 pages, $17.95

Originally published in 1968 in France, *Farewell America* quickly became a best-seller in Europe in eleven languages. Unfortunately, importation of the book into the United States through Canada was suppressed, allegedly by the FBI, because its allegations were just too hot.

Farewell America describes the roots of the Cold War, the linkage between large corporate and banking interests, the ever-growing American intelligence apparatus, and the international petroleum cartels that were lined up with a bevy of military brass and Mafia chieftains against President Kennedy. The book advances the idea that the president was killed by a combination of these powerful interests, which wanted an immediate end to the political, economic and social changes that JFK wrought. Called "The Committee," it coordinated all aspects of the murder, from setting the time and place of the shooting to the recruitment of the gunmen — possibly professional assassins selected from the ranks of Cuban exiles embittered by Kennedy's failure to intervene militarily at the Bay of Pigs — and the cover-up of the conspiracy afterward. The bottom line was that enemies of JFK collaborated with the CIA to erase the perceived Kennedy threat.

The Publishing Plot: Hervé Lamarre, the French publisher of *Farewell America*, admitted that author James Hepburn was fictitious, and that the true sources included agents of French Intelligence and Interpol. William Turner at the time was an editor at *Ramparts* magazine, which Lamarre had earlier approached regarding the English edition.

Available at fine bookstores everywhere. Or order directly from Penmarin Books for a **20 percent discount**. All major credit cards accepted.
Phone: (916) 771-5869   Fax: (916) 771-5879
Online: www.penmarin.com   E-mail: penmarin@penmarin.com

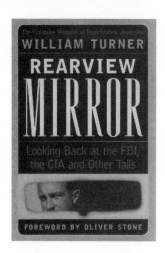

REARVIEW MIRROR
Looking Back at the FBI, the CIA and Other Tails

by William Turner
Foreword by Oliver Stone

Hardcover, 336 pages, photo insert, $24.95

[Turner's] accounts of "The Untimely Death of RFK," "The Stealth War Against Cuba," "The FBI Propaganda Machine" and more obscure events are as riveting now as decades ago. Lush, sometimes sensational conspiracy theories abound in this compelling collection. —Publishers Weekly

In *Rearview Mirror*, the explosive memoirs of investigative journalist William Turner, he revisits the significant stories and inquiries of his illustrious career, which encompasses many of the major political events of the last half of the twentieth century. In these explosive memoirs, Turner ferrets out the truth and shoots down the myths and lies promulgated not only about known events such as Hoover's FBI, the assassinations of John and Bobby Kennedy, the Bay of Pigs and Watergate, but about unknown events such as the *Farewell America* plot and the stealth war against Cuba.

William Turner began his career as an FBI agent in 1951, in the midst of the Cold War and fledgling McCarthyism. For ten years, Turner was schooled in the art of criminal and counterespionage investigations, pulling off illegal burglaries and garnering accolades from Hoover along the way. Eventually, however, he became disenchanted with Hoover's despotism, his misplaced focus on the Communist menace and his reluctance to tackle organized crime. When Turner left the FBI, he wrote the classic expose *Hoover's FBI*, and subsequently became senior editor of the radical magazine *Ramparts*, which published his eye-opening articles about the FBI, the CIA, and the police establishment, including investigations of COINTELPRO and Operation Chaos.

Available at fine bookstores everywhere. Or order directly from Penmarin Books for a **20 percent discount.** All major credit cards accepted.
Ph: (916) 771-5869   Fax: (916) 771-5879   Web: www.penmarin.com